Nothing
in This Book
Is True,
But It's
Exactly How
Things Are

Nothing in This Book Is True, But It's Exactly How Things Are

The Esoteric Meaning of the
MONUMENTS ON MARS

Third Edition

Bob Frissell

 Frog, Ltd.
Berkeley, California

Frog, Ltd. books are distributed by
North Atlantic Books
P.O. Box 12327
Berkeley, California 94712

Cover art and illustrations pp. 30, 38, 42, 66, 72, 132, 148, 164, 178 by Spain Rodriguez

Cover and book design by Paula Morrison
Typeset by Catherine Campaigne

Printed in the United States of America

Library of Congress Cataloging-in-Publication Data

Frissell, Bob, 1943–
    Nothing in this book is true, but it's exactly how things are :
the esoteric meaning of the monuments on Mars / by Bob Frissell.—3rd ed.
        p. cm.
Includes index.
    ISBN: 1-58394-067-7 (pbk.)
    1. Mars (Planet)—Geology.   2. Extraterrestrial anthropology.
3. Unidentified flying objects.   4. Occultism.   I. Title.
QB641.F75 2002
001.94—dc21

                                        2002009563

    15   16   17   18   19   /   08   07   06   05   04   03

Dedicated to my family:

To Brett,

to my parents, Elvera S. Frissell and Charles H. Frissell,

and to Joan, Joel, and Jenny.

Thank you all for your support.

Acknowledgments

Although it should be obvious from the book how much this is the work and teaching of Drunvalo Melchizedek, I would like to specifically acknowledge Drunvalo. Thank you, Drunvalo, for appearing at exactly the right time with precisely the right information and for being the perfect catalyst.

Thank you, Brett Lilly, for your enthusiasm, inspiration and support. Thank you also for putting up with my many changes during the course of writing this book.

Thank you, Alfred Lee, for all your help with the drawings. It was greatly appreciated.

Thank you, Miranda Grossinger, Spain Rodriguez, Leonard Orr, Seth Bartlett (aka Dhyana Yogi), Doug Hetchem, and Will Light.

Thanks to everyone at North Atlantic Books, including Kathy Glass, Marianne Dresser, Paula Morrison, Catherine Campaigne, and a very special thank you to Richard Grossinger, for believing, supporting, editing, *and* allowing.

Most of all, I want to thank Lois Cheesman for typing, editing, researching, co-authoring, staying up till all hours, and doing whatever else was necessary to make this book a reality.

Contents

Introduction to the Second Edition

by Richard Grossinger

In October, 1992, I reached a point I could not see my way past or through. My frames of reference–personal, relational, spiritual, cosmic–all seemed either inauthentic or futile. A new issue of *Common Ground,* the Northern California resource guide, lay on the floor in a stack of recycling papers. Without thinking that I was seeking anything concrete I picked it up and opened it almost like a game of divination. At the top of a random page was "East Bay Rebirthing Center," followed by the name Bob Frissell.

I had known about rebirthing for a long time. I had done many ritual and psychospiritual processes similar to rebirthing, and I wasn't particularly attracted to it. Yet at that moment I chose to pick up the phone and call Bob Frissell.

He lived some twenty blocks from me, just over the Oakland line from Berkeley. On the phone he was noncommital, merely scheduling an appointment. I took notes on how to get there.

I brought my dark cloud with me.

Bob said, almost immediately, "The gap between the way in which you have evolved and the way in which you haven't is getting greater and greater with the years. It is now almost large enough to kill you."

We began with his demonstrating how to breathe. He took breaths at varying speeds and in different rhythms. They all had one component; they were deep, true breaths. They were meant to be pranic winds, blowing through not just the lungs and vessel of his cellular body but his energy bodies as well. His breaths had nothing to do with hyperventilating as an altered state of consciousness. They had to do cleaning out the body, like sweeping the dust and cobwebs from a house that hadn't been cleaned in forty years. They had to do with breathing as letting go, as a trusting of one's higher self and the universe itself.

Bob wanted me to imitate his breathing. He wasn't willing to begin our work until he was sure I could do at least a passable facsimile of it.

It was incredibly difficult. Some part of me, even in my bleak mood, even with hope of release and revelation, did not want to breathe this hard.

My sessions with Bob consisted solely of this breathing. I felt like a person lighting his own pilot and then summoning a deep fire from it. When I got a blaze going, I sustained its roar as long as I could, travelling on its transformation of oxygen (and hopefully prana) into other realms and constellations. It was a delicate, porous, fluttering carpet of energy. It was usually gentle. It always made me so ravenously hungry that, either at the end of the session or during bathroom breaks, I had to coax a few almonds out of Bob's kitchen jar or a slice of bread from the wholewheat loaf sitting beside the knife next to the sink.

The breath journey always let me down gently like a parachute landing from a dream to another dream.

Bob was my guide. He said hardly anything. Mostly he might remind me to keep breathing, that is, to warn me when my breathing had gotten shallow. Otherwise, he sat there, eyes closed, travelling beside me in a parallel universe. A slow cosmic music repeating on a loop (that never seemed like mere repetition but more like a staircase headed down, down ...) guided my journeys with Bob. The shades were drawn. Babaji , Jesus, and other masters stared from posters on the walls. Their gaze was so all-knowing, it little mattered that they were mere paper replicas of faded images. They carried light. This little bit left of them recognized my higher self. Three cats bounded in and out the window and either sat on my legs or brushed by my head (as the process required). They had attended so many rebirthing sessions they knew how and when to help. They were clearly the Egyptian others of California cats.

At the end of the first session I gave Bob a catalogue of our publishing (North Atlantic Books and Frog, Ltd.). After the third or fourth session he asked me about how we ended up doing Richard Hoagland's *Monuments of Mars* and other books about the Face and City on Mars. As we talked I learned that he was involved in an esoteric tradition that reinterpreted the Face and City in light of ancient and inter-galactic events. I thought maybe he could write a book about this version of the Martian mysteries. He came to my house and, after viewing a basketball game together, we sat for hours watching Drunvalo Melchizedek lecture.

I realized that Bob stood at the juncture of two deeply sub-merged mystery churches—Leonard Orr's rebirthing with its roots in the immortal saints and yogis of India, and Drunvalo Melchizedek's sacred geometry and Pueblo millenary religion with its references to obscure branches of theosophy and uncharted bridges between science-fiction legends and sym-bolic truths masked in interplanetary tales. Bob stood there, much in the way he practiced rebirthing, as a silent guide, an intentional naif asking to be filled with higher wisdom.

Bob was also in the lineage of Christian Rosenkreutz who was invited to an alchemical wedding within a ceremony we ourselves (centuries later) still await the meaning of:

"All on a sudden ariseth so horrible a Tempest, that I imagined no other but that through its mighty force, the Hill whereon my little house was founded, would flye in pieces.... Behold it was a fair and glorious *Lady,* whose garments were all *Skye-colour,* and curiously (like Heaven) bespangled with golden *Stars,* in her right Hand she bare a *Trumpet* of beaten Gold, whereon a Name was ingraven (which I could well read in) but am as yet forbidden to reveal it."

Shaking the hill with her trumpet, she left him a letter. Trembling, he opened it to find words in golden letters on an azure field:

"This day, this day, this, this
The Royal Wedding is."

"As soon as I read this Letter," Christian Rosenkreutz tells us, "I was presently like to have fainted away, all my Hair stood on end, and a cold Sweat trickled down my whole Body."

For this was the famous Wedding, the Wedding of metal and spirit, of time and space, of Alpha and Omega, the ceremony *"unless with diligence thou bathe, /The Wedding can't thee harmless save."*

Precisely three hundred years later the alchemical wedding is located in the fragile and wounded ecology of the Earth. The tempest is now: pole shift, global warming, ozone-layer deterioration, false prophets. The Lady no longer carries a trumpet or delivers mail but speaks in riddles, through mediums and walk-ins. The Lady serves as proxy for those in the Pleiades, the Thirteenth Dimension, and among colonies we imagine on (or in) our neighboring worlds of Venus and Mars.

Leonard Orr said, "The great immortals are not hiding from us, it is we who are hiding from them."

Leonard Orr also said, "Most people love physical death more than eternal life.... [But] eternal life is pleasurable. All the immortals I have met are having a great time."

In this book Bob has told his own story in his own words. He makes no attempt to turn millennial mysteries into newspaper facts or self-help instructions. His book is called *Nothing in This Book Is True, But It's Exactly How Things Are* not because the things in it are fictive but because their essential nature is unknowable in simple time and space–not because he is satirizing New Age channelling and apocalypticism (as some reviewers mistakenly thought) but because he understands the irony of our situation trapped between the implacability of doom prophecies and the daily opportunity we have to "rebirth" not only our lives but our past histories, our fates, our loved ones, and in fact the whole cosmos. The story he tells is one of many stories and also one of many versions of one of many stories. It is a story we are living, and it is a story we are changing to such a degree that it is becoming unrecognizable even as it is being absolutely and unambiguously revealed for what it is. That is why nothing is true and yet that same "nothing" is certainly how things are. Anyone who doesn't realize this fundamental paradox of our situation is stuck in one or another prison mythology.

Rebirthing and the Flower of Life are not mythologies; they are acts conferring their own meanings. Accompanied by his feline seers, Bob himself is everyman (everywoman too), a silent spirit-guide to a journey each of us must take ourselves, a voice warning of the terrible things that will happen (but only if we addict ourselves to a vision of the terrible things that will happen).

One day I came in for a session particularly stricken and bereft. I told Bob a sad tale of stuff going wrong in my life.

I made it sound totally hopeless. It sounded totally hopeless to me as I was saying it. Then I took a deep breath, stared at Babaji and crew, smiled, and said, "But it's okay."

It wasn't just a line. I felt at that moment utterly pure in my heart and my intention to be.

"It is," Bob said, "It is okay, but only if you say so. Your word must be enough."

So I leave it with readers to decide if this is all true or if none of it is true. Because in the end your own word must be enough. For this lifetime and for all lifetimes and universes to come.

In fact, your word is the only thing that will get you through.

Richard Grossinger is the author of *Planet Medicine, The Night Sky,* and *New Moon* and the publisher of North Atlantic Books and Frog, Ltd.

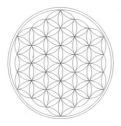

First Contact

It was January 1991. I was leading a week-long rebirthing
training at Campbell Hot Springs, Leonard Orr's center, near
Sierraville, California.

Leonard Orr is the founder of rebirthing. I spent most of
1980 training with him and have been a professional rebirther
ever since. In simplest terms, rebirthing is a tool for personal
transformation involving the conscious use of the breath and
the mind. More about that later.

I always enjoyed my time at Campbell Hot Springs. It is
680 acres of pure Sierra wilderness located right in the middle of nowhere. Just my kind of place.

In addition, there was always something special, something magical about the trainings, and this week was no exception. So if that were all that happened, I would have been
content with my stay there and left looking forward to my
next visit.

Then I met Doug!

Just prior to the conclusion of the week's events on Friday evening, I glanced at a book he left in the lunch room,
Space-Gate, The Veil Removed by Gyeorgos Ceres Hatonn.
It was full of fascinating, frightening, unbelievable information about UFOs, cover-ups, and conspiracies. I had only

a short while to glance through it; then it was time for the seminar. Guess what I was thinking about during the seminar.

As soon as the seminar concluded, there was Doug in the next room, almost as if he were waiting for me. I told him what I had seen and asked him for an explanation. We talked for hours until I was totally blown away. Then he gave me the book and a manuscript written by Bill Cooper.

> Bill Cooper is now honorably discharged from the Navy. He states that in 1972, he saw two reports relating to government involvement with alien creatures while working as a quartermaster with an intelligence briefing team for U.S. Admiral Bernard A. Clarey, then Commander in Chief of the Pacific Fleet. Bill served in that capacity from 1970 to 1973.
>
> He states that the two reports he saw were: 1) Project GRUDGE/BLUE BOOK Report No. 13 and 2) MAJORITY Briefing.
>
> The GRUDGE report he saw contained about twenty-five black and white photographs of "alien life forms" and information about them. The MAJORITY report had no photographs, Bill said, but contained information about the government's growing concern with the alien interference on this planet.[1]

Doug also said he had a number of videotapes and that he would be willing to show them to me. I stayed up most of that night reading and then spent much of the next day watching these videos.

To summarize what I learned: there was a great deal of UFO activity in the late 1940s, most of it in the New Mexico area. This included numerous incidents of downed or crashed alien craft, the most famous being the recovery of a crashed UFO on a ranch near Roswell, New Mexico, along with alleged alien bodies on July 2, 1947.

It was first announced that a flying disc had been retrieved. The cover-up began with a subsequent announcement that the wreckage was nothing but a weather balloon.

The next alleged major event occurred in 1954, when our government made contact with a race of aliens that has since become known as the "Greys." Evidently they landed at Edwards Air Force Base, met with President Eisenhower, and signed a formal treaty.

According to Bill Cooper:

> The treaty stated: The aliens would not interfere in our affairs and we would not interfere in theirs. We would keep their presence on earth a secret. They would furnish us with advanced technology and would help us in our technological development. They would not make any treaty with any other earth nation. They could abduct humans on a limited and periodic basis for the purpose of medical examination and monitoring of our development with the stipulation that the humans would not be harmed, would be returned to their point of abduction, that the humans would have no memory of the event, and that the Alien nation would furnish MJ-12 with a list of all human contacts and abductees on a regularly scheduled basis....
>
> ... It was also agreed that bases would be constructed underground for the use of the Alien nation and that 2 bases would be constructed for the joint use of the Alien nation and the United States Government. Exchange of technology would take place in the jointly occupied bases.[2]

Shortly thereafter, two outcomes became clear: 1) The Greys had ignored the terms of the treaty by abducting far more humans than they said they would. They also carried out mutilations, both human and animal. The Greys said that this was necessary for their survival, that they were a dying race and that their genetic material had deteriorated to the point where they were no longer able to reproduce. They said they needed our genetic material or they would be history. 2) Our weapons were no match for theirs. As a result, it was necessary to remain on a friendly basis with them, at least until we could develop weapons systems that might combat them. Of course, an "above top-secret" security lid was put on this with government agencies formed to investigate.

The above barely scratches the surface. There was much more information, all equally mind-blowing, as if straight out of a science fiction book.

It all had an Ace paperback quality to it. It would have been all too easy to laugh it off as the product of someone's imagination, or the hoax of the century.

But for me it fit, like the missing piece of a puzzle. It answered a lot of questions. It felt right intuitively. One of the many results of my thirteen years of rebirthing was a highly developed intuition. My intuition said yes to this and I trusted it.

Reality Check

I went back home with this new information. I was bursting with it. I couldn't wait to tell anyone and everyone who would listen. I was sure that now I had the story that everyone was waiting for, and that everyone would want to hear it, and would instantly embrace it. The cover-up would be exposed and truth and justice would be served.

I could tell you the boring details, but I won't. I could tell you how it cost me a client or two and probably a friendship or two. I could tell you how, much to my surprise, almost no one wanted to hear it. Almost—I did find a few exceptions.

I learn fast. I soon became very careful about volunteering this information, and I even began to question it myself.

I was no stranger to the possibility that what passes for truth in the mainstream media is in fact a thinly disguised veil for the real working of governments. But could it really have gone this far? Were there really little grey aliens behind the scenes giving us Star-Trek type technology in exchange for abducting some of us and genetically experimenting on those unfortunates? Could I really trust my intuition this far, or had I gone off the deep end?

I went to the Whole Life Expo in San Francisco in April 1991 and heard a presentation by two of the more moderate UFOlogists, Stanton Friedman and William Moore. They both agreed about the Roswell incident; in fact, both had researched it *ad nauseam*. However, Moore in particular went out of his way to paint Bill Cooper as a kook who could not be trusted. Was I convinced? No. Did it open up some new doubts? Yes.

I also picked up a video entitled "Hoagland's Mars: The NASA-Cydonia Briefings" and was introduced to this most interesting study regarding alleged monuments on Mars. Why hadn't the media reported on this?

I pretty much closed up shop on all of this after the Expo. There was nowhere to go with it. Besides, I had a life to live and this was getting me nowhere fast!

I did, however, connect with a group of like-minded people who met on a monthly basis. I attended a few of their meetings and received their regular mailings. In June of 1992, I received the following letter in the mail (Fig. 1–1):

DYNAMICS OF HUMAN BEHAVIOR

MADELYN BURLEY-ALLEN
FOUNDER

June 1, 1992

Greetings!

On Sunday, June 7th, I will be showing the first of five videos of Drunvalo
Melchizedak's Dallas, Texas workshop. Each video is approximately 5 hours.

> TIME: Sunday, June 7 from 1:00 - 6:00 p.m.
> LOCATION: 1710 South Amphlett Blvd.
>   Conference Room 126 on the first floor
>   This is an office complex that is North
>   of the Dunfey Hotel (Map enclosed.)

Please RSVP by Friday, June 5 as it is important for me to know who is coming and
their phone number. If I have not heard from you by the 5th, I will assume you are
not coming.

The following describes the focus of these videos:

"Resurrection, moving consciously into the next vibratory dimension can and
must be experienced and lived if we are to survive into the 21st century. Our
planet, whether you are aware of it or not, is already deep into the
transformation. The ascension process begins when a human remembers his or her
crystal energy field. There is a field of energy that is fifty-five feet around
the body that is geometrical and crystalline in nature. The remembering of this
field is triggered by a series of metaphysical drawings that are light replicas of
the 44 + 2 chromosomes in every cell of your body and specifically in your pineal
gland. This will activate a higher purpose of the pineal gland which is to allow a
forgotten ancient way of breathing to return.

This breathing is a key to higher consciousness and dimensional
translation. By simply breathing in a different way than we do now, and by
directing the pranic flow through the human crystal field, a new world will
literally open unto you. This breathing will allow you to make direct contact with
your higher Self so that trusted and clear guidance can come from within. It will
give you unparalleled protection while you are in the ascension process. It will
give you a means to heal yourself and later others. This breathing will allow you
to remember who you are and your intimate connection with God.

This video workshop is presented by Drunvalo Melchizedek. The teaching itself
comes from Alpha & Omega, order of Melchizedek and from Thoth, the Egyptian
(Atlantean), also known as Hermes of Greece, who resurrected long ago and was an
immortal that was physically living on earth until a few months ago."

I look forward to your participation. This information is extremely significant
for your ascension process.

Love and light,

Madelyn Burley-Allen

MBA:jb
Enclosure

Figure 1–1.

It seemed like an enormous commitment to sit and watch twenty-five hours of video (it actually turned out to be thirty-two hours), but I responded with an immediate yes because it seemed the perfect complement to everything I had learned in rebirthing. I had no idea what to expect; I just knew I wanted to go. The videos were from a four-day workshop entitled "The Flower of Life" led by Drunvalo Melchizedek. Was this a real person? What kind of a name was this?

What followed was some of the most engaging, enlightening, and totally mind-blowing information I had ever experienced. In addition, Drunvalo had a presence, a sincerity, a lack of judgment, a total integration of his material—the likes of which I had never seen.

I was so impressed I purchased a copy of the video, and it was my preferred source of entertainment for many weeks to come.

So what did Drunvalo have to say that was so astonishing? Well, for one, the letter's mention of breathing and ascension is what got me there, and I wasn't disappointed.

But how did that relate to UFOs and little grey aliens? And what could it possibly have to do with the esoteric meaning of the monuments on Mars?

Very good questions, so stay tuned. But first we need to look at a pair of additional riddles.

Notes

1. Linda Moulton Howe, *An Alien Harvest: Further Evidence Linking Animal Mutilations And Human Abductions To Alien Life Forms.* (Littleton, CO: Linda Moulton Howe Productions, 1989), pp. 177–178.

2. Milton William Cooper, "The Secret Government: The Origin, Identity, and Purpose of MJ-12." (Huntington Beach, CA: Manuscript copyright 1989).

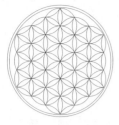

2

What's Going On?

I received two other videos from Doug. The first was a series of reports produced by Las Vegas TV station KLAS in which one Bob Lazar claimed Americans were working on alien craft at a Nevada test site called Area 51. Lazar claimed to be an ex-employee of Area 51. The craft came from the Greys.

The second was entitled "The Pleiadian Connection" and told the story of the contacts of Billy Meier with a group of beings from the Pleiades. Included in this video were a number of photos of Pleiadian "Beamships" taken by Meier.

So, was Billy Meier really being visited by the Pleiadians, or was this just his idea of a joke? There is an impressive amount of circumstantial evidence indicating he is for real. Yet Stanton Friedman and William Moore both jumped all over Meier, calling him the hoaxer of the century. And what about Bob Lazar? Is he telling the truth? If not, he certainly has an imagination. Or maybe he is one of a number of government agents purposely putting out dis-information—information, part of which may be true, and part of which is obviously false, designed specifically to lead you in the wrong direction. And if it is dis-information, what are they really hiding?

Those two videos, coupled with the Cooper and "Space-Gate" material, led me to the inevitable question: What's going on here?

I could add additional riddles. What about the crop circles? The media would have us believe that they are all the work of two hoaxers named Doug and Dave. According to Drunvalo, however, at the very minute Doug and Dave were "confessing," crop circles were being formed in Canada. It must have been the wind (Fig. 2–1).

According to Colin Andrews, a well-known "crop circle" researcher, more money is being spent on an upcoming TV documentary "proving" that Doug and Dave did it than legitimate researchers had to spend in their entire eleven years of study. Why?

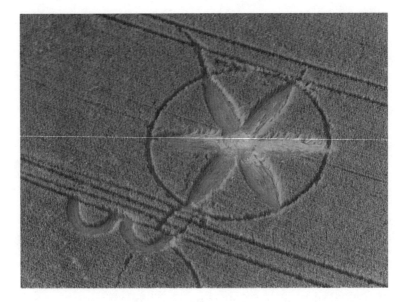

Figure 2–1. As we shall soon see, a most significant image is represented in this crop circle. Photo by George Wingfield.

And what about the monuments on Mars and the interpretations of Richard Hoagland? Why hasn't the media touched this? And what about NASA and its curious behavior?

It almost doesn't matter if any of this is true or not. Just the fact that all this information is falling around us, for whatever reason, is a clear indication that we have passed into a strange new epoch.

Another indicator of our abnormal times is the regular prophecies of Earth changes being circulated by many individuals. Gordon-Michael Scallion, for one, has predicted a most unsettling future for us. According to Scallion, we are due to experience earthquakes, volcanos, floods, hurricanes, etc., the likes of which we have never seen ... and soon. Scallion is not alone. Nostradamus, Edgar Cayce, and the Hopi Indians have all been saying similar things for a long, long time.

Obviously something is going on here on Planet Earth that is not normal, whether it is the thing being discussed or the thing it masks. As a civilization we gathered a certain amount of information since the days of Sumeria 6,000 years ago till 1900. Between 1900 and around 1950 we doubled that amount of information. Then from approximately 1950 to 1970 we doubled it again, from 1970 to 1980 again. Information now is doubling so fast that NASA is about eight years behind in getting some things into its computers so that they can use them. We are so far from catching up with ourselves that we have already entered a new phase of history while pretending everything is the same way it has always been. Not so. But read on.

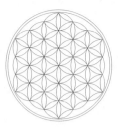

3

Why Now?

Why is all this happening now? Why not 10,000 years ago or 10,000 years into the future? It is happening now because we are at the end of a cycle and are reaching maximums on all kinds of different levels as a result. In order to explain this, I need to get ahead of my story a bit and bring Drunvalo onto center stage.

Melchizedek says that there are two motions critical to our planet. The first, familiar for millennia, is the precession of the equinoxes. The second is a wobble that was detected relatively recently. We, meaning the entire solar system, are spiraling through space in a manner that indicates we are attached to something. Astronomers noticing this began looking for that other body. It was first calculated down to a certain area of a particular constellation, then to a group of stars. Four or five years ago a specific star was targeted—Sirius A. We are moving through space with Sirius A in a spiral that is identical to the heliacal plane of the DNA molecule. We have a destiny with Sirius. As we move together a consciousness is unfolding much in the way the genes and chromosomes on the DNA molecule unreel their message from very specific places. There are key times when certain things can happen, when "genetically" critical alignments occur between

Sirius and Earth and the rest of the cosmos. One very specific alignment is now happening.

Now let us look at the precession of the equinoxes (Fig. 3–1). The Earth's axis has 23½ degrees of tilt. As the Earth goes around the sun, the axis remains tilted, giving us our seasons.

But the axis itself is in a wobble, so the axis is changing as it goes around. It changes about one degree every seventy-two years. Every 2,160 years it changes the viewpoint of one constellation, and every 25,920 years it makes one full wobble.

Over 25,920 years the tip of the North Pole traces an ellipse. At one focus of that ellipse it is closest to the center of the galaxy; at the other it is furthest away. What many ancients recognized, notably the Tibetans and Hindus, is that as we travel away from the center of the galaxy we fall asleep, and as we turn the corner we begin to wake up.

These sages of old divided the ellipse created by the precession of the equinoxes into segments called yugas. Most of the information on yugas was compiled in the last 2,000 years,

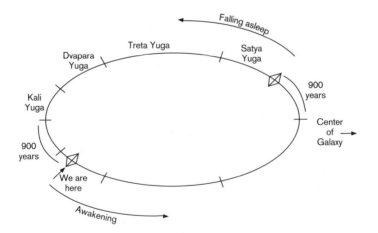

Figure 3–1. The precession of the equinoxes.

a period known as the Kali Yuga. This is coincidentally the most "asleep" point of the entire ellipse, so almost everything written about the cosmic cycle in the last 2,000 years was interpreted by people asleep trying to extract from ancient writings they didn't even understand. Then they altered these writings so that no one would find out about them. In other words, most of the information is not very trustworthy.

The ancients discovered two points located 900 years on either side of where we fall asleep and where we wake up. These points are each associated with tremendous change—changes of consciousness of beings and changes of poles on planets.

We sit now right at the turning point of beginning to move back toward the center of the galaxy and start waking up. At 180 degrees opposite the last shift, the next one is imminent. That is why we are currently approaching our limits of population and environment, among other things.

According to Thoth, whom I will introduce later, the degree of the Earth's pole shift at any time is directly related to consciousness on the Earth and how much consciousness will change. That is, there is a mathematical relationship between consciousness and degree of the pole shift. Another way to see this is that our cosmic falling asleep and waking up again are analogous to the day and night cycle of the Earth's twenty-four-hour rotation on its axis. For the most part, during the night the creatures of the hemisphere in darkness are asleep and during the day most of them are awake. So it is with the cycle of the precession of the equinoxes. During the period of time in this cycle during which the planet is asleep, the male side takes over to protect us. It is always a female who leads us back into the light. According to Drunvalo this has already happened. A woman took over sometime in February of 1989.

Though there has been great fear over the coming pole shift—certain groups of people building shelters and storing food, fearful that continents (including California) are going to be sinking, Drunvalo thinks that may not happen this time; it may be a more gentle ride. Something happened in 1972 that changed everything. More later.

Where we are in the precession of the equinoxes tells us why everything is happening now. Sometime between now and 2012, we will most likely have experienced all these events. Most likely ... but God can do anything. The other thing we must realize, according to Drunvalo, is that what is to happen will be determined by the thoughts and feelings of the people on the planet. If we change our consciousness we can change the way in which the whole drama unfolds, regardless of any prophecy.

We are creating our reality. We are creating each new collective reality every moment. Our thoughts and feelings and actions are far more powerful than we could ever imagine. For the most part, we have thus far taken little or no responsibility for them. That is changing, changing so quickly that a whole new possibility never before dreamed of is emerging.

Pole Shifts

Pole shifts are connected, if Thoth is correct, with our evolutionary pattern. They are interrelated. The last shift was a major one and directly related to consciousness. It was not a positive shift; it was a negative one, we "fell" in consciousness.

Up until just recently, I think somewhere around 1950 or so, it was thought that polar shifts were something that never happened, or if they did it was once in a billion years and never again. But in fact the poles shift every 12,500 to 13,000 years, or in other words, every time we come to these particular points in the precession of the equinoxes. So it happens on a regular basis. Scientists are now finding that there indeed have been many pole shifts in the history of our planet.

Not only do pole shifts happen regularly but the poles have even reversed themselves, north to south and vice versa. Pole caps have been at the equator. There is hardly anywhere on the planet where you can't find sea shells. You can find them on the top of the Rocky Mountains; you can even find them in Lake Titicaca, which was all below sea level at one time and is now over 12,000 feet high. Much of this information was discovered by scientists taking six-inch, eleven-foot-long core samples out of the ocean floor and reading the sediment just like tree rings.

Pole shifts are big. From methods of ionium and radiocarbon dating there is evidence to suggest that approximately 12,000 years ago the North Pole shifted from the Hudson Bay, or 60 degrees North Latitude and 83 degrees West Longitude, to its present location in the Arctic Ocean.[1]

Right now we are physically on the line between the constellations Virgo and Leo. When we look out into the heavens we see ourselves traveling from Pisces into Aquarius but we are physically in Virgo going into Leo. This is why the Sphinx is a virgin and a lion together, the symbols for Virgo and Leo.

John White provides considerable data on this subject in his book *Pole Shift.* In northern Siberia, there is evidence of humans, bison, and trees, all shredded and ripped apart with incredible force and then instantly frozen solid. The bison had tropical food in their stomachs when they were frozen solid. It should be noted that there are more than 200 different kinds of ice formed as the temperature drops quickly. These relics are so deep down into the ice structure that this food is still edible today, 12,500 years later. Pole shifts happen very quickly. In fact, they complete themselves in about twenty hours.

There are all kinds of theories as to why pole shifts occur. For instance, the ice caps expand and slip, causing the Earth to go off balance just like a gyroscope. A more modern theory, from the work of the Swedish physicist Hannes Alfvenis, is called magnetohydrodynamics or MHD. This theory proposes that beneath the Earth's solid crust there is a semi-solid layer. Sometimes this layer acts as a solid and keeps the Earth's crust in place and at other times, notably when there is a collapse of the Earth's magnetic field, this layer acts as a liquid allowing the Earth's crust to shift position.[2] A replica of this has been demonstrated in laboratories.

Nobody really knows what triggers the process. Once it begins, the surface of the Earth moves at about 2,000 miles per hour and the winds approach 1,000 miles per hour. Obviously, that is enough to devastate just about anything on the surface. It is no wonder we hope this time to be able to do it with a little more control.

However large the pole shift may be, there will be a change in consciousness associated with it. That is, we will shift at the same time. If we make a bigger consciousness change we can affect the physical pole shift even more. Our task, then, is a matter of becoming conscious enough to control the way the next pole shift happens so that it is enjoyable rather than fearful.

As a rebirther, let me say that a pole shift is just like birth. If a woman is in a state of fear, then giving birth will be difficult and painful. If she is relaxed and has no fear then the birth happens easily. Birth can and should be easy. Either way, it is all a function of consciousness.

You might consider this information frightening. Don't be afraid. On a deeper level you already understand that there is no problem. Usually, when a planet experiences a pole shift, the prognosis is that many are called and few are chosen. Eventually everyone makes it, though. A few people initially attain Christ-consciousness and the rest drop down a dimension or two (which to them feels harmonious). Over a long period of time, probably hundreds of thousands of years, the few who made it bring the rest of the planet back and eventually the whole planet goes into Christ-consciousness. But here right now on Planet Earth something else is happening. I will lay this out in upcoming chapters.

Notes

1. John White, *Pole Shift* (Virginia Beach, VA: A.R.E. Press, 1980), p. 94.

2. John White, *Pole Shift*, p. 149.

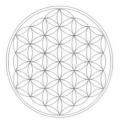

4

Problems With Planet Earth

When it's time for consciousness to make a big shift, there is a simultaneous dying and a birth process leading up to the actual shift. Planet Earth has major problems right now, much more severe than we are being told by our governments. Starting somewhere around 1989 the powers-that-be began to release the crucial information, but only in segments. If any one of these problems reaches its crisis point, all life on the planet will be severely threatened. And they are all coming to a head.

For example, around 1980 Jacques Cousteau claimed that the Earth's seas and oceans were dying. At first nobody took him seriously, but by 1990 the Mediterranean Sea was 85 percent dead. The Atlantic Ocean is not far behind. The Pacific is doing a little better because it is a larger body of water.

If the oceans die, so will the plankton and phytoplankton. They are not only a cornerstone of the food chain but a major source of oxygen on the planet as well.

Another problem is the destruction of the Earth's ozone layer, allowing the entry of more and more of the sun's deadly ultraviolet rays. This has been called one of the biggest dangers humanity has ever faced by the Director of the United Nations Environment Programme.[1]

21

Destruction of the Earth's ozone layer is occurring on an extreme and unprecedented scale. It is occurring at a much greater rate and over a much wider area than scientists predicted. Ten to 20 percent of the ozone layer was destroyed over Europe from December 1991 to February 1992, the highest amounts ever.[2] Joe Farman, the British scientist credited with the discovery of the Antarctic ozone hole in 1985, said that the seasonal losses of ozone above North America could reach 20 to 30 percent by the year 2000.[3]

The problem will continue to worsen over the next one or two decades because of past emissions of chemicals that have not yet reached the upper atmosphere. In ten to twenty years there may not even be an ozone layer. And we cannot live without it.

These are just two of the many environmental problems we face. There are so many going on right now that we seem to occupy a sinking boat. A particular aspect of planet Earth, this third-dimensional aspect which we call our daily lives, will not be intact much longer.

According to Drunvalo, if you were to return here in just a few years you would find the planet dead on a third-dimensional level. But life would still exist on Earth; we are all going to shift up in wavelength to another place that is prepared for us, which is beautiful and where there are no problems. We will move into a slightly shorter wavelength and a higher energy vibration. The Bible refers to this state as Heaven. Actually, we will be going from the third to the fourth dimension.

According to Drunvalo, extraterrestrials regularly visit a planet like ours. But it is against universal law for them to interfere with us. For this reason they enter one overtone higher than the one the planet sits on so that they are invisible to us. But they can monitor us very clearly from this higher overtone. In fact, the next higher overtone on our planet is right now so full of vehicles filled with curious occupants that more recently arriving visitors have had to go into the second overtone, and they have now almost completely filled that one. Ours is the most unusual situation ever known in this universe. There are even beings from distant galaxies here to watch. Usually they would *never* bother with us. Most of the ETs who are here are not only in light bodies but they are of such a nature that their ship and their body are one and the same.

Notes

1. "OZONE, Making a Killing: How Workers And The Planet Are Disregarded ... at Du Pont"; a pamphlet published by Greenpeace, 1436 U Street, N.W., Washington, D.C. 20009, April 1992.

2. "Ozone levels found to be lowest on record," *The Independent*, London, United Kingdom, April 8, 1992.

3. Joe Farman, European Ozone Research Coordinating Unit, United Kingdom Department of Environment Press Conference, October 15, 1991.

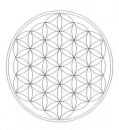

5

Dimensions

All dimensional levels of this world are here and present right now and interlinked. The only difference between dimensional worlds is their wavelengths. Wavelength is the key to the entire universe. We live in a reality created solely by wavelength. The wavelength of our third-dimensional world is 7.23 centimeters.

Dimensions are separated from one another by wavelength in exactly the same way as the notes are on a musical scale. Each tone on the scale sounds different because of its wavelength. Any octave on the piano has eight white keys and five black keys, which together give its player the chromatic scale. The thirteenth note is actually the first note of the next octave, and these octaves keep repeating themselves in either direction. In between each note and the next are twelve harmonic, holographic points; in dimensional terms these are the overtones. It is also the same as changing channels on a TV set. When you operate the channel control, you are tuning to different wavelengths.

There is a voidness between dimensions like the voidness between two notes. There is a greater void, a great wall if you will, between octaves. Each dimension is also separated from the others by a 90-degree rotation. If you could change wavelengths and rotate 90 degrees, you would disappear from this world and reappear in whatever dimension you were tuned to. The images you see looking out from your eyes would change according to the wavelength of the world you had entered. This planet has many different worlds; they are all right here, but our consciousness is tuned to one particular wavelength. Meanwhile, we literally exist on multiple dimensional levels and our experience on each level is completely different.

For example, if we were to go up one level, which we are in the process of doing, we would find that whatever we think, as soon as we think it, instantly manifests. Here, by contrast, on the third dimension, there is a time delay. Even though our thoughts create our reality unerringly here as well, their manifestation obviously is not instant.

The key to understanding how to move from one dimensional level to another begins with locating an electromagnetic field shaped in the form of a star tetrahedron. That field is around our bodies.

The Merkaba

A star tetrahedron is made up of two interlocking tetrahedrons in a manner that resembles the Star of David but three-dimensionally (Fig. 5–1). The two interlocking tetrahedrons represent male and female energy in perfect balance. The tetrahedron facing up is male, and the one facing down is female. There is a star tetrahedral field around everything, not just our bodies.

There is also a tube that runs through the body. It connects the apexes of this star tetrahedral field. Learning how to breathe through this tube, combined with rotating the fields, produces the merkaba, a vehicle of ascension.

Figure 5–1. A star tetrahedron.

We have a physical body, a mental body, and an emotional body and they all have star tetrahedral shapes. These are three identical fields superimposed over each other, the only difference among them being that the physical body alone is locked—it does not rotate. The merkaba is created by counter-rotating fields of energy. The mental star tetrahedral field is electrical in nature, male, and rotates to the left. The emotional star tetrahedral field is magnetic in nature, female, and rotates to the right. It is the linking together of the mind, heart, and physical body in a specific geometrical ratio and at a critical speed that produces the merkaba.

The word "Mer" denotes counter-rotating fields of light, "Ka" spirit, and "Ba" body or reality. So the Mer-Ka-Ba then is a counter-rotating field of light that encompasses both spirit and body and it is a vehicle—a time-space vehicle. It is the image through which all things were created, a geometrical set of patterns surrounding our bodies. That image begins at the base of our spine as small as the original eight cells from which our physical bodies first formed. From there it extends out a full fifty-five feet in diameter.

Again, the counter-rotating fields of light of the merkaba comprise a time-space vehicle. Once you know how to activate these fields you can use your merkaba to travel throughout the universe.

On most terrestrial people the merkaba is not functioning. Drunvalo says there are about 2,000 people on this planet whose merkabas are functioning, and about 8,000 ascended masters who reside on another level of the Earth's consciousness.

Melchizedeks

Even though you may travel in the merkaba to other dimensional levels, if your consciousness is not developed enough to handle the higher vibrational levels you will not be able to stay there. Certain beings, however, have managed to move through all the dimensional levels and remain conscious.

The act of learning how to be stable and conscious in all 144 dimensional levels (the twelve dimensions and the twelve harmonic overtones of each of them) teaches them how to go across the great wall and into the next octave. The person then comes out the other side and sees the big picture, with the realization that all of creation repeats itself over and over.

At that point they have a decision to make—to go beyond creation and back to the source, or to remain here. If they remain, they are called Melchizedek. Life then uses them to heal inter-dimensional problems.

Currently there are about ten million Melchizedeks in the galaxy, and there are five on planet Earth.

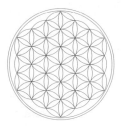

6

Our History

In order for us to understand what is happening now and what will happen in our future, it is essential that we know the past. Plants, for instance, use a mathematics described by the Fibonacci sequence to determine what to do in their growth. A plant looks back to see what it just did, ascertains where it is now, and then knows where it is going. It adds the number of leaves it just grew to its present complement to know how many leaves to grow next. It says, for example, I just grew one leaf and I am at one, so that means I now grow two. When it gets to two leaves it says, I was just at one and I just grew two more, so now I am at three, and so on. It needs to look back to see what it just did combined with where it is now to know where to go. Such is organic structure.

As humans we have to know our history because we have to know how we got into our present predicament in order to get out of it. We think that our history began in 3800 B.C. in Sumeria and that nothing came before that except hairy barbarians. We assume we are the greatest thing that ever lived on this planet. In truth, according to Drunvalo, there have been civilizations so far ahead of us that we can't even imagine them. Civilizations on this Earth go back 500 million years. The planet is a star seed to which external life forms have come from all over, combined with each other, generated new life forms, and left. Each of the life forms they created have gone through five levels of consciousness. Right now we are on the second of the five.

Almost all the evidence from past advanced civilizations has been put out of context or ignored. For instance, we have a connection with the star Sirius about which little is known but which is essential to understanding our present plight. Robert Temple's book *The Sirius Mystery*[1] presents the following: There is a tribe near Timbuktu in Africa called the Dogon. For more than 700 years this group has had information that presumably it cannot have—information our scientists have had for only the last twenty years or so.

The Dogon know about the star Sirius in detail. Sirius is the brightest star in our sky, situated to the left and straight down from the belt of Orion. The Dogons said that there was another tiny star rotating around Sirius and made of the heaviest matter in the universe. This star completed its rotation once every fifty years. It was a very old star. Because scientists couldn't see this star through our telescopes, ethnographers thought it was just Dogon mythology. In 1970 a photograph was successfully taken of a white dwarf star rotating around Sirius. Like the one in Dogon "myth," it is a very old star. One cubic inch of it is estimated to weigh 2,000 pounds. The orbit of the star was calculated to be 50.1 years. This star was named Sirius B and the original Sirius renamed Sirius A.

When a team of scientists visited the Dogon tribe to find out how they knew about this, the elders said that a flying saucer landed. Beings emerged and made a large hole in the ground which they filled with water. The occupants, who looked like dolphins, jumped into the lake they had made, then came up to shore, and talked to the Dogon people. They told them that they were from Sirius and related many Sirian stories.

The Dogons had an even more incredible bit of information. They had a visual image of the movement of Sirius A and Sirius B from Earth for the time period between 1912 and 1990, culminating in an exact image of where these stars would be at this time. They also had a great deal of information about the planets in our solar system, including various moons. How did they know or imagine this so specifically?

My next bit of information has to do with the Sphinx. Egyptologists say that the Sphinx was built around 2500 B.C. by the pharaoh Chephren. In his book from 1961 called *Le roi de la theocratie pharaonique (Sacred Science)*, the mathematician, philosopher, and Orientalist R.A. Schwaller de Lubicz says:

> We have to acknowledge that a great civilization must have preceded the vast movements of water that passed over Egypt; it is this which is implied by the existence of the sphinx sculpted in the rock on the western cliffs at Giza, this sphinx whose whole leonine body, with the exception of the head, shows an indisputable water erosion.[2]

An Egyptologist named John Anthony West, after reading Schwaller de Lubicz' book in 1972, decided to research the weather patterns found on the Sphinx. He saw that the wear patterns were excessive, up to twelve feet deep in the back. He brought in an American geologist, Robert Schoch, to look at it from a geological point of view. He discovered beyond any doubt that the patterns were not the result of wind and sand but water. It was calculated that there would have to have been a minimum of 1,000 years of torrential rain flowing on the Sphinx consistently for it to have been worn to these patterns. Geology now stands in direct contradiction with archaeology. The Sahara Desert is at least 7,000 to 9,000 years old, which means the Sphinx has to be at least 8,000 to 10,000 years old, minimum.

Egyptian archaeologists have nothing to say about this. The evidence is overpowering that it is true, but it threatens to break down all our concepts of who was on this planet when we believe that there was no one here capable of building something like the Sphinx 8,000 to 10,000 years ago. According to Thoth the Sphinx contains proof of 5½ million years of civilizations on this planet, even though there have been more like 500 million years of civilization. Something happened 5½ million years ago that broke the Akashic record memory of this planet. Even Thoth doesn't know what it was and doesn't know how to get through to the older records.

The Sumerian civilization seemed to arise overnight with no evolution at all. The same is true for Egypt. Egyptian writing appeared one day in its most developed form and went downhill after that. All the ancient civilizations—Sumeria, Babylonia, Egypt, and so on—developed quickly and went downhill immediately. In the ruins of Sumerian cities archaeologists have found tablets which depict the Solar System, listing the planets in their correct order. One even gives the distances between the planets.[3] How did anyone know this? They also provide detailed records concerning the precession of the equinoxes. It has been calculated that the only way to discover the precession of the equinoxes is from observation, and that the minimum time of observation would have to have been 2,160 years. How did the Sumerians have this information, when, according to our way of thinking, there was no advanced civilization 2,160 years before them?

Our Creators

Now my discussion will drop back about 400,000 years in our history. Here I will incorporate information from both Thoth and Zecharia Sitchin, in particular Sitchin's books *The 12th Planet*[4] and *Genesis Revisited*.[5] Sitchin believes that there is another planet in our solar system, the Sumerian Nibiru, which has an elliptical orbit similar to that of a comet. It takes 3600 years for the planet to make one complete circle of the sun. The people on this planet, called the Nefilim, came to Earth over 400,000 years ago; Thoth doesn't say why, in fact he never mentioned the Nefilim by name. He only told Drunvalo that there were giants on the Earth at the time (the Nefilim ranged from ten to sixteen feet in height). Sitchin claims the reason was that they needed gold for their atmosphere. In *Genesis Revisited,* he writes:

> On their planet Nibiru, the Anunnaki/Nefilim were facing a situation we on Earth may also soon face: ecological deterioration was making life increasingly impossible. There was a need to protect their dwindling atmosphere, and the only solution seemed to be to suspend gold particles above it, as a shield.[6]

So they came here to mine gold. After 200,000 years or so of enforced labor the miners rebelled and decided to create a subservient race—which is us—to mine the gold for them. It is notable that in southern Africa in the oldest known gold mines, archaeologists have found the bones of *homo sapiens* and artifacts that go back at least 50,000 to 100,000 years. Sitchin asserts that the Nefilim created us about 300,000 years ago, but Thoth is very exact. Thoth says we were created exactly 200,209 years ago (from 1994).

Sitchin theorizes that the Nefilim created us through genetic experiments, but according to Thoth the Nefilim couldn't do that alone. They had to have help from outside the Solar System. That external help came from a familiar source. The Sirians joined with the Nefilim to create us. The Nefilim first landed in the ocean and emerged as half-men and half-fish. They went underwater initially to make contact with the dolphins, who were on a similar consciousness level with them. They had to check in and get permission to do what they wanted to do. According to the Sumerian records, the Nefilim first went to southern Iraq and built their cities. They then went to southern Africa to mine gold.

The Sumerian records are round clay tablets that came out of the ancient Sumerian cities, the cities mentioned in the Bible. These records, discovered only in the last century, are the oldest sources of information, bar none, on the planet. Sitchin is one person who has the ability to interpret these records.

Again, Thoth just said there were giants and that they became our mother. He said that seven of these beings dropped their bodies and formed spheres of consciousness. They merged into the seed of life and created an ovum. When seven beings link together geometrically in this way to form the seed of life, a flame appears, four feet tall and of bluish-white light. It is cool but looks like a flame. This was then set in the "Halls of Amenti."

The Halls of Amenti are a very ancient place, built more than 5½ million years ago. No one knows how old the Halls of Amenti really are or who erected them, because of that event 5½ million years ago that broke the Akashic records of the planet. Remember—even though history on the planet goes back 500 million years, we have access only to the last 5½ million years.

The Halls of Amenti are actually a dimensional warp in space resembling a womb. There is only one way in, but once you get there it is like being in infinite space. Such a warp sits always one dimensional overtone higher than the vibrational level of the Earth. It is located usually 440,000 miles out in space, but during the era of Atlantis it was on the surface of the Earth. Now it is 1,000 miles inside the Earth. Drunvalo has been allowed into the first room where there is a pyramid. Inside the pyramid is a golden mean room made out of stone. In the middle of the room is a cube. On top of the cube is the flame.

Simultaneous preparation for this creation or trans-semination was being made on Sirius B, or, more precisely, the third planet out from Sirius B. Sixteen males and sixteen females who comprised a married family there traveled to Earth from Sirius B and went directly to the flame in the Halls of Amenti. They lay down and merged with the flame. Their conception period here was 2,000 years. These two separate races were involved in our creation—one from Nibiru and one from Sirius.

Thoth said we were originally placed on an island off the coast of southwestern Africa called Gondawanaland. He said we were placed there primarily so we could not leave. We were there 50,000 to 70,000 years. From there we were brought to southern Africa. Interestingly enough, African creation stories all agree on one piece of information. They all say they came from an island off the southwestern coast of Africa, called Gondawanaland.

According to Sitchin's interpretation of the Sumerian texts in *The 12th Planet,* after the Nefilim created us to work in the gold mines in Africa, some of us were brought to Mesopotamia to help in the gardens in E.DIN. The "gods" loved us because, after all, we were made in their own image. But in the garden in E.DIN where the Nefilim had their orchards we were told not to eat the fruit of a certain tree— called the tree of knowledge. We disobeyed. Eating this fruit and gaining its "knowledge" was sigificant because it gave us the ability to reproduce sexually. Up until this point we were hybrids, a cross between two different species, and like all hybrids we were incapable of reproduction. Sitchin interprets the Sumerian texts as saying we are a cross between the Nefilim and *Homo erectus,* the predecessor of *Homo sapiens.* It is through Thoth that we get the additional information about the role of the beings from Sirius.

Not surprisingly, the Nefilim did not want us reproducing. They wanted to maintain control of their own experiment. The knowledge we gained from eating the fruit was not scientific as such—it was the knowledge of how to procreate, how to turn ourselves from sterile hybrids into a new species fully capable of reproducing. The Nefilim were angry when we gained the ability to reproduce, and they made us leave the garden. According to scholars of ancient texts, the Sumerian records precede the Biblical records, and the Biblical creation stories seem to be just a summary of older Sumerian texts.[7]

Although we had to leave their garden, the Nefilim allowed us to grow food on our own. We went to the mountainous area east of the gardens in Mesopotamia. According to Thoth, we remained there for a long time. But then there was a big shift in consciousness and another pole shift, and Gondawanaland sank. Many of the survivors went to Africa, but the most evolved went to Lemuria, a land which rose above water when the other continent sank.

Lemuria

The continent of Lemuria lasted for 60,000 to 70,000 years. During the era of Lemuria the consciousness of the planet became predominantly intuitive and female. The Lemurians had technology that we can't even begin to understand—for example, dowsing rods that work only when your mind and heart link together.

Jumping ahead in time to Lemuria approximately 80,000 years ago, or about 1,000 years before the continent sank—and the continent was sinking very slowly almost from the beginning—there lived a couple by the name of Ay and Tyia. Ay and Tyia had become physically immortal beings during the course of their lives and so they opened a school to teach immortality and ascension to others—the Naacal Mystery School. Ascension is a method of consciously moving from one world to another, taking your body with you. It is different from resurrection, which is consciously moving from one world to another by dying and then reforming your light body on the other side. In the course of its existence, the school graduated about 1,000 immortal masters right up until the time when Lemuria was sinking rapidly. Extremely intuitive, the Lemurian race knew the land was submerging; they were well prepared for it, so there were probably very few casualties. As the continent became uninhabitable, almost everyone from Lemuria migrated to a zone as far south as Lake Titicaca in Peru and as far north as Mount Shasta in California.

Atlantis

As Lemuria sank, the poles shifted, and the land mass of Atlantis arose. The thousand or so immortal masters of the Naacal Mystery School of Lemuria went to Atlantis, specifically to one of its ten islands called Undal. When they got to Undal, the first thing the masters did was build a wall right down the middle of the island from north to south. This wall, which was about forty feet high and twenty feet wide, sealed off both sides so you could not cross from one to the other.

Next, these immortal masters erected a smaller wall from east to west, thereby dividing the island into four quadrants. This structure replicates the human mind, which is divided into two hemispheres with the corpus callosum running down the middle. The left hemisphere, the male side, is based on logic. The right hemisphere, the female side, is based on experience or intuition. But the male side also has a female, or experiential, aspect associated with it, and the female side has a male, or logical, aspect associated with it. These are the four quadrants of the human mind.

When the masters had completed the division of their island, half of the 1,000 immortal masters went to one side of the island and the other half went to the other side. The masters on the left side became logical thinkers and the masters on the right side of the island became intuitive thinkers. They carried this out to the point that the island became alive. They then projected onto the main island the ten patterns of the Tree of Life, so that vortexes of energy began to rotate out of these ten spots and summon the Lemurians to Atlantis. Each person was drawn to the specific vortex that was associated with his or her true nature. The Lemurians who had settled from Lake Titicaca to Mount Shasta didn't know why, but they suddenly felt the need to migrate to Atlantis. They were drawn there by the energy vortex created by the immortal masters.

Unfortunately, the evolutionary pattern of Lemuria was such that the Lemurians had only developed the nature of eight of the ten vortexes associated with the Tree of Life. The Lemurians migrated to eight of these ten spots, which became major cities, but the remaining two vortexes were left vacant. This is where a big problem first began.

The vacant energy vortexes ended up pulling in two uninvited extraterrestrial races that then joined with our human consciousness and became part of our evolutionary pattern. The first extraterrestrial race was the Hebrews, whose origin was unknown, and they were not a problem. In fact, in many ways they helped because they brought in advanced information that we didn't yet have. The problem was with the second extraterrestrial race sucked in. Specifically, this race came from Mars—not the Mars that we now know or that existed then, but the Mars of approximately one million years ago. At that time Mars was a beautiful planet, totally alive, not dead the way it has become. But the Martian inhabitants were suffering from, and in fact the planet was being destroyed by, the effects of a "Lucifer" rebellion stimulated by the same type of sickness we would later encounter. But the Martian problem was not created by Lucifer himself—rather from a similar type of character. I'll call this general problem "the Lucifer rebellion," even though Lucifer himself was only involved in the most recent upheaval.

The Lucifer Rebellion

Lucifer was one of the most incredible angels that God ever made. He had a flaw, however; he thought he was as good as God. Lucifer knew the creationary pattern, the merkaba, but it was originally intended to be enacted only internally. Creating it internally meant you had to have your emotional body intact along with your mental body, which protected you. Lucifer went one step further. He dared to do the obvious and created it externally. By separating himself from God, the source, he was in fact not able to do it internally. Yet initially, prior to the consequences, he thought, "No big deal. He does it internally, I'll do it externally. Same old merkaba." This is like saying the hydrogen bomb is the same as love because it is bright and hot. Externalizing the merkaba was a billion times more serious.

Now this type of experiment against God had been attempted three times before the one that affected our planet, and it always ended in total chaos. The last Lucifer rebellion was about 200,000 years ago and at the time he convinced about a third of the angels to join him.

About a million years ago the race on Mars was dying from the effects of an earlier Lucifer rebellion (the third one). The planet was terminating from merkabas run amok. When you create a merkaba internally using love or your

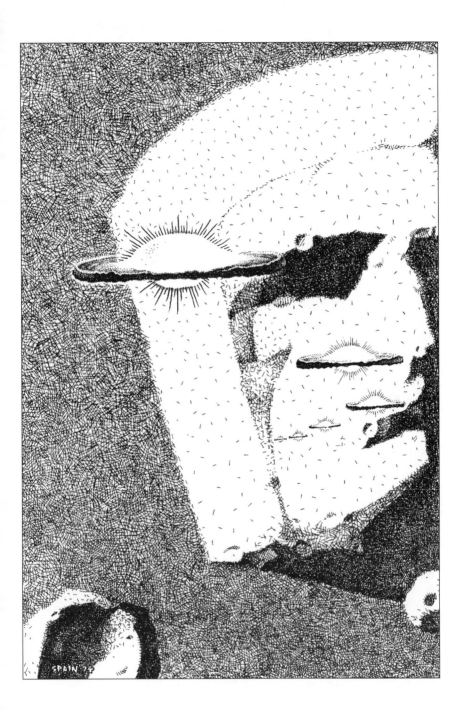

emotional body, it becomes a living field around your body, but when you create it externally you don't have to use love—you only have to use the calculating mind. Ultimately, this act produces a being with only a left brain who doesn't have an emotional body or understand love. The best example of such a race is the Greys (the Greys are descendants of the Martians and one of the alien races now visiting the Earth). Another effect of creating the merkaba externally is that the act itself is generative of duality. How could it not be, since it dualizes in order to externalize and turn emotions into technology. Once everything is dualized and running on motors, it becomes more and more difficult to perceive the One spirit that moves through everything. So we see good and evil and, even though the One spirit is still present in an externally created world, it is incredibly difficult to discern.

When the Martians came to Atlantis they imported the effects of the Lucifer rebellion right along with them, and this is the deed that led to our downfall on Earth. The problem was that Mars was a full left-brain culture; the Martians knew and understood everything intellectually but they had no feeling; specifically, they had no love. They had no reason to care for anyone other than themselves. As a consequence they were always fighting, and they destroyed their atmosphere just the way we're doing here. As Mars was dying a small group of Martians, approximately 1,000 or so, built structures in the region we have come to call Cydonia—the massive humanoid face and the monuments the *Viking* spacecraft photographed on Mars in 1976. These monuments represent in exquisite mathematical detail at many levels the form of a star tetrahedron inscribed in a sphere, and they also describe how the Martians created their own unfortunate external merkaba. They had lost the ability to create an internal merkaba so long ago they didn't know what it was. After all, such a vehicle requires an emotional body. They certainly knew how to create an external merkaba and they did just that. They got in it and left, believing that was their only option.

Through the creation of this elegant external time-space vehicle, the Martians were able to journey into space, travel in time, and discover and decide the perfect time and place for them to enter. They saw, projected far ahead into their future—about 65,000 years in our past—this place on planet Earth on Atlantis, so perfect and waiting for them. That is where they headed. They stepped in against our will and tried to take over immediately, but there were too few of them and they failed. They finally decided to go through the motions of trying our feminine way even though they didn't understand or accept it. But they put on a good act. They tried it, in fact, for 50,000 years but always with disruptions. Their influence on us was so strong we began to switch our consciousness from a female to a male orientation. We didn't transmute completely, but we were significantly distorted.

When the Martians stepped into our evolutionary pattern in Atlantis we were about the equivalent of a thirteen- or fourteen-year-old girl and they were the equivalent of a sixty-five-year-old man. They stepped into our evolutionary pattern against our will and, essentially, raped us. As I said, they would have taken over if they could have, but there weren't enough of them so they had to go along with our ingenue program at least for a while.

Even though there were always conflicts, things progressed fairly smoothly until roughly about 16,000 years ago. At this time a comet hit planet Earth where Charlestown, South Carolina, is today. Remnants of the molten stone scattered over an area the size of four states, making huge impacts. The Atlanteans were an extremely advanced culture at that time, so they knew the comet was coming. In fact, they had the technology to blow it out of the sky. The Martians advocated using the machinery to destroy the intruder, but even though they had a strong influence on us, our female orientation was still strong enough for us to say no. Basically, the intuitive aspect said, "No, don't shoot it out of the sky: it's God and what will be will be, so let's just let it happen." So the Atlanteans watched the comet hit and, guess what, most of the damage occurred right in the area where the Martians were staying. In fact most of that area totally sank. For the remaining Martians, that was the last straw.

The devotees of the external merkaba decided from that time on they would not follow our lead anymore and would go their own way. What they did was to assemble another Luciferian experiment just like the one carried out a million years ago on Mars that resulted in the external vehicle. They still did not have the requisite emotional body and love necessary to create counter-rotating fields as a living entity, for they had done nothing to nurture this aspect of themselves on Earth. They had, or at least they thought they had, the ability to reinvent the merkaba externally. In so attempting to create it, they intensified the pathology of the Lucifer rebellion on Earth and they also failed miserably. The experiment lurched out of control and began to rip open the dimensional levels, causing spirits who were not meant to be here—spirits who had been consigned to other dimensional worlds—to come in by the millions. This blew the lid off things; the place just got crazy.

Picture thousands upon thousands of yowling, terrified, highly psychic, telekinetic entities whipping through not only the atmosphere but the mind, body, and spirit of the inhabitants. It wasn't pretty.

The ascended masters helped a great deal by sealing up most of the dimensional tear as quickly as they could, but with millions of these disembodied beings already present, every Atlantean had anywhere from twenty to a hundred spirits in their bodies. Things in Atlantis got much worse than they are here now, though we are fast approaching that. And those spirits are still here. Everyone on this planet has at least a few of them living in their bodies.

This failed experiment happened about 16,000 years ago, and for the next 4,000 years matters just kept worsening. The ascended masters, our highest aspect, the very highest degree to which consciousness on this planet has reached, looked outward from their habitats on the tenth, eleventh, or twelfth overtone of the sixth dimension and prayed for help. They had to find a way to rescue everyone. They couldn't just get rid of the Martians or kill the disembodied spirits; that is not what ascended masters do, it is not the path of life. So what the ascended masters were looking for and praying for was help in finding a win-win situation for everyone.

In the highest aspects of life there is unity consciousness, and in unity consciousness there is no duality, no illusion. It is abundantly clear there is One spirit that moves through everything, and since the One spirit moves through every-thing, then everything is a part of the whole. This is precisely why the ascended masters couldn't just obliterate the Mar-tians. Our modern surgical philosophy of excision—to cut you up and take out what isn't working—is not what true life is about. By annihilating the Martians or driving them off, a loss for anyone would ultimately have been a loss for everyone.

A lot of intergalactic consuls were involved in the ensu-ing deliberations. They looked back into the remote past and were able to see something that had been done before and in fact had worked. It required synthetically initiating plan-etary Christ-consciousness. Not merely allowing it to pro-ceed naturally but synthetically beginning the process of creating the Christ-consciousness grid on the planet, with the result that everything would eventually be healed.

Once our consciousness reaches a certain level all the problems solve themselves. Christ-consciousness is unity consciousness, so, if it could be achieved, everyone would win.

There are five levels of consciousness associated with planet Earth. The levels of consciousness are directly related to the number of chromosomes we have in our genetic makeup. They also each prescribe a range of height. The first level of consciousness has forty-two plus two chromosomes, and this is harmonic with unity consciousness. At this point collective consciousness operates such that if one person experiences something, it is possible for everyone else to access this memory and relive it. This is the dreamtime of the Aborigines in Australia. The range of height associated with this level of consciousness is three-and-one-half feet to five feet.

The second level of consciousness is where we are now. We no longer have this unity consciousnes; we are cut off and separated. The second level of consciousness has forty-four plus two chromosomes, and the approximate range of height is from five feet to seven feet.

In the third level of consciousness, which is Christ-consciousness, there are forty-six plus two chromosomes. The range of height is from ten to sixteen feet. Here we are back into unity memory again, but its form in the third level is upgraded into one of instant manifestation; it is no longer dreamtime but realtime. When you remember something it is real. It is not just your memory but the memory of all Christ-conscious beings who have ever lived. At the third level there is really only one consciousness that moves through everything; its key is memory. This is what immortality is all about. Immortality is not living in a body forever because there is always some place higher to move. The key is not having a break in consciousness as you move through the different levels, not having a memory loss, being able to leave when you want and continuing to know where you've been.

The fourth level of consciousness has forty-eight plus two chromosomes and a height range of twenty-five to thirty-five feet. The fifth level has fifty plus two chromosomes and a height range of fifty to sixty feet. The fourth level is disharmonic like the second but it is a necessary step to get to the fifth and highest level that can be achieved on this planet.

Thoth

Thoth is a specific historical man who went through ascension 52,000 years ago. For 16,000 years he was the king of Atlantis, where his name was Chiquetet Arlich Vomalites. He remained on Earth in the same body until May 4, 1991. He could have left earlier—many ascended masters have— but he was among a small group who decided to stay. Knowing without any doubt whatsoever that all things are interconnected and that there is One spirit that moves through everything, Thoth preferred to remain here as a teacher.

He did leave for about 2,000 years and traveled to various planets. He would arrive at a planet and sit there for a hundred years or so, observing and learning how the inhabitants did things. Then he would go to another one, until he finally returned here. His vow was to remain here on Earth until we reached a certain level of consciousness. We have now reached that level, so Thoth left this planet on May 4, 1991.

Evidently, what happened before, during, and after the Gulf War was a culmination of something. The light on the planet is now stronger than the darkness for the first time in 16,000 years. Even though we don't see it yet, the power balance has shifted and the laws have reversed themselves. Now when negativity resists the light, which is its very nature, instead of overpowering the light it gives more power to the light and we get stronger. So hang on!

Thoth's most famous act was introducing writing to the planet. He was called "the scribe" in Egypt, for he is the one who wrote all the ancient history down. That is why Drunvalo was sent to him. Most of Drunvalo's information about us and our history comes from Thoth. Thoth was always quick to point out that he may not have it 100 percent accurate, but his account is probably pretty close to what actually happened.

Drunvalo first met Thoth in 1972. He was studying alchemy—that is, how to turn mercury or lead into gold—not for the purpose of making money but to observe chemical reactions. All chemical reactions have parallels in life somewhere on one level or another. By understanding chemistry and the way atoms combine to form molecules, and how these molecules recombine, you can see in tiny detail how larger operations happen. True alchemy is primarily understanding how our level of consciousness goes into Christ-consciousness.

Drunvalo was studying this system with a master. One day they were doing an open-eye meditation. After one hour, Drunvalo's teacher disappeared from the room. In two to three minutes a completely different body formed right in front of Drunvalo. This person was short, about five-feet-three-inches, and he looked about seventy years old. His appearance was ancient Egyptian and he wore very simple clothing. Drunvalo especially remembers his eyes, which were just like a baby's, very soft with no judgment.

He told Drunvalo there were three atoms missing in the universe and he wanted Drunvalo to find them. Drunvalo had an experience, which he will not describe, in which he understood what was meant. Thoth bowed, said thank you, and disappeared. A few minutes later the alchemist teacher reappeared. He knew nothing of this; in fact, he thought he had been there the whole time.

Drunvalo didn't know then that the person that appeared to him was Thoth, and he didn't see him again until November 1, 1984. At that time they began to communicate regularly over several months.

Anyway, to get back to the story, Thoth together with Ra and Araaragot, who were also former kings of Atlantis, got the blueprint for the Christ-consciousness grid and went to Egypt. They went to Egypt (which at the time was known as Khem) because the flame which contained the ovum of our collective consciousness had an axis point which emerged there. Someday the grid associated with that point would mature as Christ-consciousness. They drilled a hole straight down the axis, which extends through the Earth, to the ovum of our consciousness. This axis comes out in Egypt and also on the other side of the Earth in Moorea, a small island near Tahiti. Thoth says that there is a vortex or spiral on both ends of the axis and that a shadow of it formed on the ground would look like a logarithmic spiral (Fig. 6–1). They then built three pyramids on that spiral.

The primary purpose of the pyramids was to move our consciousness from the second level (where we are now), to the third or Christ-consciousness level.

It was an instrument for planetary initiation, designed specifically to take a forty-four plus two chromosome person into Christ-consciousness and stabilize him.

According to Thoth, the pyramids were built with the mind and heart, manifested from memory on the fourth-dimensional level. They were constructed in a period of three days, from the top down. They linked the very consciousness of our evolutionary pattern with the logarithmic spiral. Deep below the pyramids they laid out a small temple city which

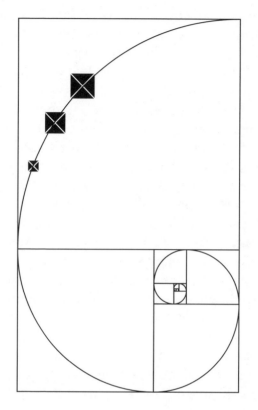

Figure 6–1. The logarithmic spiral on the Giza plateau.

held about 10,000 people and which, by the way, is still there.

Every single species of life form on the planet has a grid connected with it. Even if that species exists on only one spot on the Earth, its grid extends around the whole planet. These grids subtend an average of sixty feet from inside the Earth to about sixty miles above the Earth. If you were to see them superimposed over each other it would look like a light, white-blue haze coming off the Earth.

The most intelligent, advanced, oldest life form on this planet is the whales. Next are the dolphins, then humans. We think that we are the most advanced, but the whales and dol-

phins are far, far beyond us. We think we are the most
advanced because we can create external things. That, however, is an impact of the Lucifer rebellion brought from Mars.

The most advanced life forms do not create externally.
They create everything they need internally.

The whales have been on this planet, conscious and alive,
for 500 million years. They hold the memory of the planet.
This is what the movie *Star Trek IV* was all about. Without
the whales we would have no memory, we would be lost.

The dolphins have been around here for at least 35 million
years. They even came out and walked on land for a while and
decided against it. Dolphins' flippers have hands inside them,
human hands. These creatures are amazingly aligned with
humans. They are mammals, not fish, and both sides of their
brains function at 100 percent. When they sleep, they turn off
half of their brain. We have only half of our brain working at
any time; the other half is shut down. Of the half that is on,
only about 5 to 10 percent is used. So from the dolphins' per-
spective, we are not only asleep, we are also unconscious.

There are three grids for human consciousness around
the planet. The first one is forty-two plus two; the one we are
in now is forty-four plus two; and, as of February 4, 1989,
there is also the third grid, which is the Christ-consciousness
grid of forty-six plus two. Without that grid, no planet can
go into Christ-consciousness.

This then is what Thoth, Ra, and Araaragot were prepar-
ing. They were beginning to do geomancy on the surface of
the Earth to create the Christ-consciousness grid synthetically, which would, in turn, give us the vehicle to move into
the next higher level of consciousness.

So this trio made a hole aligned directly with the invisible axis of our consciousness ovum. Then they laid out three
pyramids, a major project of geomancy. Subsequently they
situated 83,000 sacred sites throughout the planet. These

were created totally on the fourth dimensional level, so don't sign up with any travel agencies advertising tours in New Age directories. Then over a period of 13,000 years they drew humans from every race and all walks of life to build the requisite church here and pyramid there to establish an operational pattern on each of these sites. Scientists may yet discover that all the sacred sites on the planet are laid out in either logarithmic or Fibonacci spirals, mathematically connected and delineated back to that single spot in Egypt. The area in Egypt, only recently discovered, is now called the solar cross. The Association for Research and Enlightenment in Virginia considers this to be one of the most critically important places in Egypt.[8]

In addition to what the masters did in Egypt, they also bequeathed us the second level of consciousness, the one we are now on, as an intermediate disharmonic step toward the third—or Christ-consciousness—level. They accelerated this by introducing writing, which caused us to lose our dreamtime or unity memory. Prior to this, writing was not necessary because recall was total and instant. The second level of consciousness, the disharmonic stage that we are now in, intervenes because life has not yet figured out how to go directly from the first to the third level. However, the second level is a tier that one wants to get on and off as quickly as possible because if a civilization stays on it too long, its planet runs a high risk of destruction. We can't get off this level any too soon.

The complex in Egypt I've been describing was built about 200 years before the deluge and the shifting of the axis. This, by the way, was THE flood, the one in which Noah floated off in the ark and survived. Immediately prior to the shifting of the axis and the deluge, Thoth flew to the Sphinx. This marks the oldest object on the planet which, in actuality, lies about one mile beneath the surface and is a very large spaceship. Thoth presented this along with much of the information found in this chapter in an ancient document called *The Emerald Tablets.*

According to Thoth, the spaceship is used to protect us. He says every time we approach a pole shift we become extremely vulnerable because we go through a three-and-a half-day period when the magnetic field of the planet collapses. At this time the dark side always comes in and tries to dominate. This has happened like clockwork throughout our 5½-million-year history; but each time one very pure person has found the ship and lifted it into the air, and whatever this person thinks or feels happens. It must be a person who has stepped into Christ-consciousness, so that what they think and feel in fact does manifest instantly. This act always prevents the dark side from taking over.

As we are again approaching a pole shift, the spaceship has already been put into place. In 1989, a woman from Peru crossed into Christ-consciousness, raised the ship, and thought the following: the Greys are suffering from a terminal illness found only on Earth. And remarkably, this is what immediately began to happen. By the end of 1992 the Greys, to a one, were gone. Their only recourse was to blast out of here; they couldn't live on Earth anymore.

Back to the craft—I don't want you to have any misunderstanding. This spaceship is only three to five atoms thick, and is flat on the top and bottom, about two city blocks across, and round. It is designed to attach to and run off of your own merkaba. Usually it is one overtone higher than whatever one the Earth is on, and that is how it is able to be located one mile beneath the planet's surface.

After the Martians' failed experiment on Atlantis, there were approximately 4,000 years of life on Earth getting more and more chaotic. The Earth came to the time in the precession of the equinoxes and readiness for a pole shift,

approximately 12,500 years ago. Thoth raised the ship, flew
back to the island of Undal on Atlantis, and picked up about
1,600 ascended masters. They had gotten no more than a
quarter of a mile off the ground, Thoth said, when Undal
sank. That was the last part of Atlantis to go under. Thoth
and the ascended masters then traveled back to the Great
Pyramid, as the magnetic field of the Earth collapsed. The
collapse lasted for three-and-a-half days. It took our memory with it. Our collective memory is directly dependent upon
the magnetic field of the Earth, so if it collapses, we have no
idea of who we are. It's back to savagery. But if you have
mastered the merkaba you can create your own magnetic
field from the counter-rotating fields of light and retain
memory.

The masters landed on top of the Great Pyramid, which
was constructed in such a way that it created a perfect landing platform for this spaceship. There they formed a merkaba from which a large counter-rotating field of energy
extended 1.6 million miles into space. For the critical three-
and-a-half-day period during the pole shift the masters controlled the axis, the tilt, and the orbit of the planet. In fact,
they changed the orbit; it used to be a 360–day periodicity
and now it is 365 and a quarter days.

The masters stayed in this ship for the period in which the
magnetic field was collapsed, and at the end of it they found
a whole new world. Atlantis was gone, portions of what is
now the United States had risen above water, and the planet
was on a different, much lower, dimensional level. That's
why archaeologists can't find any evidence. They are looking at the wrong vibration.

The masters entered the Great Pyramid by a circular tunnel leading to its underground city. Ra took about one-third
of them there—Tat, Thoth's son, among them. The people
in this underground city later formed the Tat Brotherhood,

and there is a large community of immortal beings living there to this very day.

The ship then flew to Lake Titicaca and the Island of the Sun. There Thoth disembarked with about another third of the masters, and they founded the Inca empire. The ship next journeyed to the Himalaya where Araaragat disembarked along with a little less than one-third of the masters. The rest of the ascended masters (seven of them) returned to the Sphinx, raised the ship in its overtone so it could pass through the Earth, and then descended about a mile below the surface into a circular room where the ship itself remained until 1989.

These three places—the underground city, the Island of the Sun, and the Himalaya—were chosen for very specific reasons having to do with planetary geomancy as set up by the masters for a synthetic Christ-consciousness grid of the Earth. The Egyptian aspect became the male point of the grid; the Mayan-Incan aspect became the female counterpoint of the grid; and the Himalayan aspect became the neutral or child point of the grid.

Egypt and Stair-Step Evolution

Egypt became the home not only of the Tat Brotherhood, but also many of the survivors of Atlantis. Having had their memory erased by the pole shift, the Atlanteans had reverted to barbarianism, reduced to the basic survival skills of building a fire to stay warm and so on. They had to wait a long, long time until they could even begin to develop again. In fact, it wasn't until about 3,800 B.C. when the Nefilim began to reestablish their terrestrial connections in the place where they had set up their original bases in southern Iraq. The Nefilim simply gave back the lost information.

There is a clear discrepancy between what Thoth says and

the writings of Sitchin regarding the development of the Egyptian civilization. Sitchin believes that the Sumerians brought their culture to Egypt, but Thoth says no—it was our own ascended masters, the Tat Brotherhood, who established the Egyptian civilization.

In both Sumeria and Egypt, then, there was an amazing correspondence. Each culture came out in its fullest and finest form virtually overnight. Then, both cultures began to degenerate from there.

Attaining full bloom overnight is roughly equivalent to a modern-day automobile suddenly appearing in 1903 with no prototype. Archaeologists have absolutely no explanation. Sitchin, in *The 12th Planet,* calls Sumeria "The Sudden Civilization."

The Tat Brotherhood closely monitored the Egyptians. When they felt the time was right, they sent out their own members dressed exactly like the Egyptians and began to re-seed the knowledge of Atlantis. This is called stair-step evolution. There are no evolutionary patterns; all of a sudden the people just know everything about a certain subject. Then there is a little plateau, and all of a sudden they know everything about another subject, and so on.

As soon as a particular piece of information was given it would almost immediately begin to degenerate. The explanation for this lies in the precession of the equinoxes. As we move away from the center of the galaxy in this 26,000–year cycle, we fall asleep. After the last pole shift the Earth was simply at the point in the precession of the equinoxes where planetary consciousness must fall asleep. Thus, each time new information was given, the people almost immediately began to lose it until about 500 B.C., by which time the Egyptian civilization was almost totally gone.

Figure 6–2. Akhunaton. "The Coronation of Akhunaton" from *Akhunaton: The Extraterrestrial King* by Daniel Blair Stewart.

Akhunaton

The Egyptians also began to lose the idea of one God or One spirit that moves through everything and to worship many gods. The ascended masters addressed this problem with another direct intervention. They decided to have a Christ-consciousness being walk on the very surface of the Earth to put the real thing back into the Akashic records.

This Christ-consciousness being was named Akhunaton (Fig. 6–2), who, by the way, was not from the Earth but from the star system of Sirius. He developed a whole new religion, the religion of the sun. That is, the sun was worshipped as a unity image.

Akhunaton was only given seventeen-and-a-half years

around 1355 B.C. to make his imprint. In the meantime everyone hated him. He disrupted all the religions, telling people that the priests were not necessary, that God was within
them, and that all they needed to do was learn how to
breathe and everything would be fine. Even though Egypt
had the strongest army in the world, Akhunaton, who was
a pacifist, told them they couldn't fight anymore. He ordered
them to stay within their borders and respond only if
attacked. The people despised him because they adored
their religions, even though they were a mess of contradic-
tions. Akhunaton told them henceforth there would only be
one religion for the whole of Egypt, and no one wanted to
hear that.

Akhunaton gave initiates a twelve-year advanced training of the "missing knowledge" (I will describe this school
in more detail later). This course produced almost 300 Christ-
consciousness beings.

These immortal beings were almost entirely women. Until
roughly 500 B.C., they joined with the Tat Brotherhood and
remained in the underground city beneath the Great Pyramid. Then they came out from under the Great Pyramid and
migrated to Masada, where they became known as the Essene
Brotherhood. Mary, mother of Jesus, was one of these immortal beings.

The Egyptians disposed of Akhunaton after a seventeen-
and-a-half-year reign. Then they did what they could to erase
the memory of him. Everything reverted back to the old ways.
In spite of this, Akhunaton was ultimately successful. He
wasn't after a lasting legacy, not on a planet drifting into
sleep. All he needed to do was to get his example into the
Akashic records, the living memory of the Earth. He needed
to establish the Essene Brotherhood, which would suffice to
get the next stage going. He did exactly what he was supposed to do, in the time he was allotted.

Notes

1. Robert Temple, *The Sirius Mystery* (New York: St. Martin's Press, 1976).

2. John Anthony West, "Civilization rethought," *Conde Nast Traveler,* February 1993 (New York: Conde Nast Publications, Inc.), p. 102.

3. Zecharia Sitchin, *Genesis Revisited* (New York: Avon Books, 1990), p. 15.

4. Zecharia Sitchin, *The 12th Planet* (New York: Avon Books, 1976).

5. Zecharia Sitchin, *Genesis Revisited.*

6. Ibid., p. 19.

7. Eberhard Schrader from *Die Kielschriften und des alte Testament,* quoted by Zecharia Sitchin, *The 12th Planet,* p. 209.

8. The Association for Research and Enlightenment was founded to preserve and continue the research of Edgar Cayce.

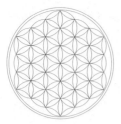

7

Drunvalo

Just who is Drunvalo Melchizedek? Let me begin by telling you about Drunvalo's great-great-great-grandfather, Machiavinda Melchizedek. Machiavinda was the person assigned from Galactic Center to be with us. He has been here from the very moment we were created.

The Great White Brotherhood and what you might call the Great Dark Brotherhood are two bodies of consciousness opposed to each other in every imaginable way. Machiavinda was from the Great White Brotherhood. The Great White Brotherhood does everything it can to advance our evolution, while the Great Dark Brotherhood does everything it can to induce fear and delay evolution.

The forces of these two brotherhoods tend to balance each other out so that our evolution takes place at exactly the right time, neither too soon nor too late. Viewed from a higher level—the fourth dimension or above—this is unity consciousness. The two brotherhoods are just different aspects of the One working in harmony. It is only because we are down here in the midst of polarity consciousness that we see it in terms of good and evil. Evil may do some amazingly harsh and disgusting things, but at the level of polarity consciousness, these are mere lessons.

Due to amazing events which happened in 1972 (I will devote a whole chapter to this later), the Great Dark Brotherhood, who, by the way, knew what was going to happen, enlisted four additional members from the star systems of Orion, while the Great White Brotherhood sent four of their own in response to this. Drunvalo was one of the four. He was chosen because of his longstanding experience in the Melchizedek Order in the thirteenth dimensional realm. He had been there almost from the beginning, or about 10 billion Earth years. He had almost no awareness of polarity consciousness and was dispatched here because of that, because of his innocence.

Drunvalo came as what is called a "walk-in." Another person occupied his body until Drunvalo was ready to use it. That person undertook certain training and schooling that Drunvalo was later able to use. This was all done by agreement. It is illegal, according to universal law at the highest level, to take over a body any other way. The person who left his body for Drunvalo to occupy was given something very special. Drunvalo did not say what it was other than that.

Drunvalo can remember almost every minute of coming through the dimensional levels, from the thirteenth all the way down to the third dimension, to get here. However, he purposely placed a veil over his memory of the thirteenth dimension. According to him, to have memory now of life in the thirteenth dimension would be just too painful. There is no way you could exist here on the third dimension and maintain full memory of what the thirteenth dimension is like. He does remember being on the thirteenth dimension and being asked by his father to come here, and he also recalls being given a movement pattern to move inside the Great Void, which is what he had to go through to get here.

He moved in this pattern through the Great Void for a long time. He doesn't know how long it was in Earth time, but it was a long time, perhaps millions of years. He continued to move until light reappeared, and at that time and place he was met by Machiavinda. Then he went through the center of a nebula, the middle star in the belt of Orion. This is one of the primary star-gates to other dimensional levels. For instance, there are thirteen different star-gates in our galaxy, but the middle star in the belt of Orion is a special one. At this star-gate, great light and great darkness operate very close together. Many of the Greys emanate from precisely this part of the galaxy.

After going through the belt of Orion, Drunvalo headed for the Pleiades. His goal was a particular fourth-dimensional planet with a green atmosphere. He had no form on this planet but he was totally conscious; or, put differently, his form was just a ball of light. He gestated in a baby's body and kept it for about fifteen Earth years. He soon learned that the Pleiades contain a galactic university. Its inhabitants dwell on the higher overtones of the fourth dimension, and all learning there is accomplished through pleasure and joy. All teaching utilizes games.

When Drunvalo learned what he needed to know on the Pleiades he flew to the third planet out from Sirius B. This world is almost all ocean. The Sirians are also on the fourth dimension, but on a lower overtone of it than the Pleiadians. They do not yet experience joy and pleasure to the same degree as the Pleiadians, but they are getting there. On this marine planet Drunvalo had no body—he was just consciousness. Here he existed by attaching himself to a very large being, a female orca whale. He swam with this whale for about one year, and while he swam with her she told him the history of the Earth. She had the total memory pattern of the planet Earth inside her.

This joyous interlude ended when three humanoid fourteen- to sixteen-foot-tall Pleiadians came to him and said it was time to go. They took Drunvalo to the land mass of the planet he was on and gave him an already-made adult male Sirian body. ("People most places in the Galaxy don't waste bodies the way we do," Drunvalo has remarked.) Its cells contained the memory patterns of how to run the Sirian ship he was then given.

Drunvalo, along with 350 crew members, took this Sirian ship with a prepared flight pattern for Earth. This involved flying from Sirius B right through the middle of Sirius A. You pass through successfully simply by tuning to the same vibration as the sun so that "hot" is no longer hot. Ninety seconds later you come out through the Earth's sun. This is because of our intimate connection with Sirius. Using this maneuver, Drunvalo and crew reached the orbital field of Venus, the world containing the Hathor race, the most advanced beings in this solar system.

After some adventures in dimensional reality on Venus (the travelers encountered torrential sulphuric-acid rain), they transited to Earth and came in one overtone higher than our own dimensional level so we could not see them. Drunvalo left his Sirian body and ignited into a ball of light. This still felt like a shift in consciousness to him, in other words, easy, before his more rude introduction to real polarity consciousness. He shifted upward into the Earth's fourth dimensional level and from there kept climbing dimensional levels looking for a trace of life. Nothing in the fourth. The fifth was an utter state of vacancy. He finally found the ascended masters hanging out on the tenth, eleventh and twelfth overtones of the sixth dimension. He joined them and learned from them for a period of time from 1819 to 1850.

In 1850 Drunvalo was born as a female into the Taos tribe in New Mexico. He maintained this woman's body for forty years, and in 1890 he left it consciously just by holding her breath. He returned to the sixth dimensional level and stayed this time until 1972.

On April 10, 1972, Drunvalo walked into his current body. It was all done in one breath. The spirit leaving breathed out and Drunvalo breathed in. That was it, clean and legal. The two spirits had been talking for seven to nine years before this and they petitioned for and got full permission to do this on all levels.

Drunvalo doesn't tell these stories about himself to prove he is anyone special. To the contrary, it is to serve as a reminder to you, to show how special you are. Consider, for example, the possibility that *you too* are a higher-dimensional master here on special assignment. Consider also that in order for you to properly do your job, it was necessary to become as human as possible; that is, to go to sleep and forget, and at the proper time you would be reminded of your true nature. You have done the first part perfectly. Now it is time for phase II.

Drunvalo *does* remember and that is the difference. He is here as a catalyst to provide us with that necessary wake-up call.

existence now was accomplished through this pattern. Contained within the flower of life is everything. There isn't anything in the universe and never will be that isn't manifested in that image—all languages, all laws of physics, all biological life forms—including all of us individually.

Thoth told Drunvalo that he would find this image in Egypt. Drunvalo wondered about this because he had never seen anything like it in all his Egyptian studies. However, soon thereafter, a friend returning from a trip to Egypt gave him a picture that contained the flower of life depicted on the wall of a structure about 6,000 years old, located in one of the oldest temples ever discovered in Egypt.

The image is called the "flower of life" because its replica originates in a tree. Think of a fruit tree: as it grows, it flowers and then fruits. The fruits fall, and in each one is a thousand seeds, and each seed has in it the image of the tree. Contained within the geometry of the flower of life is all of creation.

The seed aspect delineates the first circle and the six circles around it (Fig. 8–2). The next image is the tree of life (Fig. 8–3). Its image is contained in the seed. When you superimpose the two images (Fig. 8–4), the seed of life and the tree of life, you see how every line links and the tree fits perfectly inside.

Another central image in sacred geometry is the *vesica piscis* (Fig. 8–5). The *vesica piscis* is simply a circle next to another circle exactly the same size so that the edge of one circle passes through the center of the other. The common area created is the *vesica piscis.* Two equilateral triangles fit inside this image and two squares, which form a rectangle, fit around it (Fig. 8–6).

The flower of life and the seed of life are nothing but *vesica piscis.* Also, looking at Fig. 8–4, you will see that every line in the tree of life is either the length or width of a *vesica piscis.*

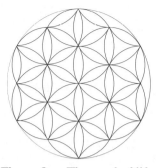

Figure 8–2. The seed of life.

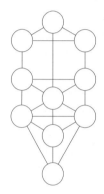

Figure 8–3. The tree of life.

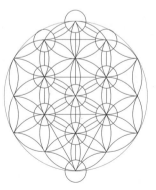

Figure 8–4. The seed of life and the tree of life superimposed.

The nature of sacred geometry is that it is absolutely flaw-less, there are no accidents. It continues to unfold until the entire universe is created. Every single part of it is interlinked with everything else. You can start at any point and gener-ate the whole language of creation.

Of all the things Thoth taught to Drunvalo, he considered the knowledge of sacred geometry to be the most significant. It might be difficult for us to conceive of geometry as being the base of creation, but this is simply how things are. There is nothing on any level of existence whatsoever that doesn't have geometry behind it. To understand how the actual geom-etry works is a crucial first step in convincing our rational minds of the reality of the One spirit that moves through everything.

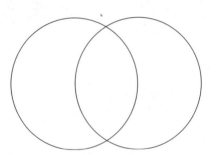

Figure 8–5. The vesica piscis.

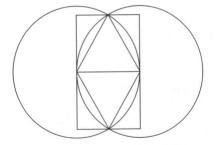

Figure 8–6. Two equilateral triangles fit inside and two squares, which form a rectangle, fit around the vesica piscis.

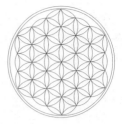

9

The Right Eye of Horus

I myself was aware of integration leading to unity consciousness. In fact, I had been teaching it for years. It is the goal of rebirthing.

I was aware of immortalist philosophy and of ascension. I had been consciously moving in that direction for years.

I was aware of the existence of light forces and dark forces. But something was missing.

Even after I discovered Drunvalo through the videos and even though he was answering a multitude of questions, there was still something missing!

For a long time I did not pay any attention to the sacred geometry presented by Drunvalo. I had trouble even feigning interest in it. It took time and patience to work my way into it. Sometimes it took hours to fully understand one drawing, as I only had the videos to learn from. It turned out to be worth every minute of the effort, however.

I now think it is the most important information I have learned. Coupled with my previous training and knowledge, the study of sacred geometry has allowed left- and right-brain integration to take place.

Even though I had been deeply involved in intuitive spiritual integrative work for many years, there was an internal

73

conflict. My right-brained feminine side intuited the One spirit and unity consciousness, but could not prove it. My left-brained male side was of no help whatsoever. It did not believe it, and saw duality everywhere.

So I was in a sort of limbo. Even becoming more conscious through the years didn't do it and in some ways seemed to make it worse. That of course is the very nature of healing—that anything you are holding onto that is less pure than your highest intentions will come to your attention, and as long as you stay conscious, you will move through it. I knew that, but just knowing didn't help.

The Right Eye of Horus and the sacred geometry contained within it was the missing information I was unknowingly seeking.

Drunvalo says that the purpose of this information is the integration of the left and right brain. It is about "convincing" the left brain or the male side of us that there is One and only One spirit that moves through everything. Once the left brain is convinced, then integration begins to take place, and we begin to move from polarity into unity consciousness.

So, what's the significance of all this? Well, for one, we can't make the jump to the fourth dimension until this integration has taken place. On the fourth dimension, manifestation is instant. Reality there is whatever you think it is, manifesting instantly before you. It would seem then that unity consciousness and purity of thought would be rather important there.

But they are important here, too! Your reality *here* is whatever you say it is and it appears before you, even though there is an apparent time lag on the third dimension.

We won't know for sure about the fourth dimension until it has become our moment-to-moment living-presence reality. Our current reality is right here and now. In order to create it to the best of our ability, it is very useful to know as much as we can about integration and unity consciousness so we can bring more of that higher-dimensional light and wisdom down here.

In that spirit I invite you to engage in the following material. Get a compass and ruler if you wish, and do the drawings yourself. Have fun!

The Law of One

During Akhunaton's time in Egypt, he gathered together a few thousand people, all of whom were at least forty-five years of age. They had been through twelve previous years of training known as the Left Eye of Horus, which is an emotional body right-brain training. Akhunaton took these people for another twelve years through his Egyptian Mystery School, The Law of One, and gave them the missing knowledge. This was later transmitted to Drunvalo by Thoth.

The actual map appears in only one place, underneath the Great Pyramid in a long hallway leading into the Hall of Records. All the chromosomal images of the sacred geometry are on the upper part of the left-hand side of the wall. This information was otherwise only transmitted orally.

The symbol for Akhunaton's school was the Right Eye of Horus, which is controlled by the left brain. This is male knowledge, the logical side of how everything was created by spirit and nothing else, for spirit needs nothing to create the universe.

Following are the first three verses of Genesis, Chapter One:

> In the beginning God created the heaven and the earth. And the earth was without form, and void; and darkness was upon the face of the deep. And the Spirit of God moved upon the face of the waters. And God said, Let there be light: and there was light.

One thing the Bible left out and which Akhunaton's school very clearly specified was that in order for spirit to move in the Void it had to move relative to something. The Great Void is total nothingness; if all that is there is spirit and it moved but had no point of reference, how would you know it moved? The way Akhunaton's school analyzed this was as follows: spirit projected itself out as far as it could go in all six directions—up and down, forward and backward, and left and right (Fig. 9–1). This can be conceived on three axes marked x, y, and z. The amount of projection is irrelevant; even if it were only one inch it was enough.

So spirit projected itself in six directions. Its next step was to connect the lines—first to form a square (Fig. 9–2), then

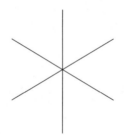

Figure 9–1. Projection of Spirit in six directions.

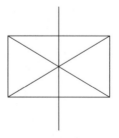

Figure 9–2. Square.

to form a pyramid (Fig. 9–3), and then to bring the lines down into a pyramid below, which was an octahedron (Fig. 9–4). Now spirit had the reality of an octahedron around it. Even though it was just a mental image, movement was now possible because perimeters had been established.

Spirit then began to rotate the three axes, thus tracing the image of a sphere (Fig. 9–5). In sacred geometry a straight line is considered male and any curved line is female. Thus, by rotating the octahedron on its axis, spirit went from being male to being female, i.e., the sphere. The Bible reports that the male was completed first and the female second. This is a movement from straight lines to curved lines. The reason spirit went from straight lines to curved lines is that the

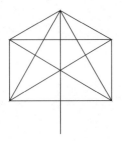

Figure 9–3. Pyramid.

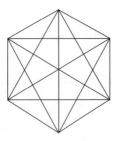

Figure 9–4. Octahedron.

geometric progression necessary for creation is much easier from the female curved lines.

So now the spirit of God finds itself inside a sphere. *Genesis* says, "The spirit of God moved upon the face of the waters," but where to? In the entire universe there was only one new place and that was the surface. So the student in Akhunaton's school was taught that spirit moved to the surface. Anywhere on the surface, it doesn't matter where. The first motion out of the Great Void is to move to the surface (Fig. 9–6). After that first motion everything else is automatic; every motion from there on shows you exactly where to make the next motion until the entire universe is created.

The third verse from Genesis is: "And God said, Let there be light: and there was light." After moving to the surface

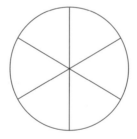

Figure 9–5. The image of a sphere.

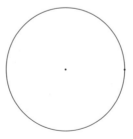

Figure 9–6. The first motion out of the Great Void
is to move to the surface.

there is only one thing to do, and that is to make another sphere (Fig. 9–7). What you have then is a *vesica piscis,* or two interlocked spheres, which *is* the metaphysical structure behind light. And that was the first day of Genesis. Where the two spheres come together is a circle or oval. By moving to this new circle and making another sphere you get the next image, which marks the second day of Genesis (Fig. 9–8). Now a rotational motion begins to happen on the surface of the sphere until it completes itself. This is all automatic. See Figures 9–9, 9–10, and 9–11.

When you get to the sixth day of Genesis you have six circles fitting perfectly with nothing left over (Fig. 9–12). On the seventh day spirit rests, because the genesis and all the laws of the universe are now complete. As the image continues to rotate in a vortex, three-dimensional objects start to come out of the pattern.

It is important here to understand that sacred geometry is not just lines on a page; rather, it is the sacred motions of spirit in the Void. It is the map of movements necessary to get out of the three-dimensional Great Void in such a way that, in our case, we end up on planet Earth. Depending on which dimensional overtone you are on, there are actually 144 different forms of voidness.

The first image to come out of this pattern is a tube torus (Fig. 9–12). It emerges from the first rotation or the first six days of Genesis. You create this image by rotating the pattern (when you rotate the pattern, you get a tube torus with an infinitely small hole in the center). Remember, it is a three-dimensional shape, not a two-dimensional one. The tube torus (Fig. 9–13) is the primal shape of the universe. It is unique in that it moves in on itself; there is no other shape that can do that.

Stan Tenen,[1] through more than twenty years of research, tracked the spiral of a tube torus out of the middle and took

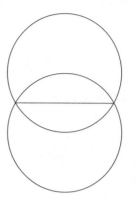

Figure 9–7. The first day
of Genesis.

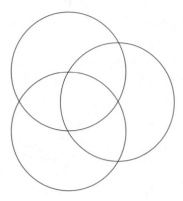

Figure 9–8. The second day
of Genesis.

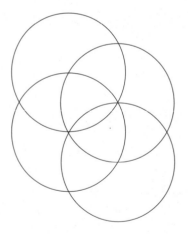

Figure 9–9. The third day
of Genesis.

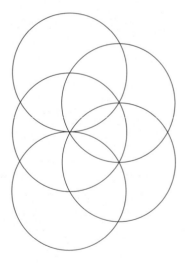

Figure 9–10. The fourth day
of Genesis.

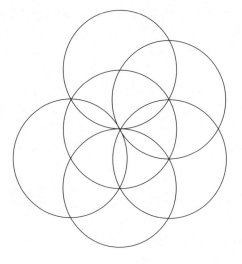

Figure 9–11. The fifth day of Genesis.

Figure 9–12. The sixth day of Genesis.
The seventh day was a day of rest.

out the shape. He removed the minimum amount of matter to delineate the tube torus and placed it inside a three-dimensional tetrahedron (Fig. 9–14). He found that by shining a light through it so that the shadow of that shape came out onto a two-dimensional surface he could generate all the letters of the Hebrew alphabet, exactly as they are written and in order. He also found that by changing the shape to a different position he could project all the Greek letters. Then by changing the position again he could configure all the Arabic letters. He did this simply by moving this particular shape to different positions inside a three-dimensional tetrahedron. There are actually twenty-seven primary symmetrical positions inside a tetrahedron.

Figure 9–13. Tube torus.

Figure 9–14. The spiral of a tube torus inside a tetrahedron.

So the first thing to come out of Genesis is the connection of metaphysical form to language. And this all occurred during the first seven days of creation.

So we have begun a rotational vortex energy pattern. Every time a new rotational pattern is completed a new form is produced and that new form is the basis of creation. The rotation always begins at the innermost places (Fig. 9–15). The next rotation is shown in Figure 9–16. By erasing some of the lines in Figure 9–16, you will come up with Figure 9–17, or the "egg of life." This is a two-dimensional depiction of a three-dimensional figure. The egg of life is actually eight spheres, the eighth lying directly behind the middle sphere. The egg of life is the pattern through which the harmonics of music, as well as of the electromagnetic spectrum, are connected, and it is also the pattern that underlies all biological life. It is the pattern of all structure, no exceptions whatsoever.

The next rotation gives you the outline—that is, the correct number of circles—for the "flower of life" (Fig. 9–18). This flower contains seven circles as shown in Figure 9–19. Figure 9–20 presents how the flower of life is usually depicted. It has

Figure 9–15. The innermost places.

Figure 9–16. The next rotation.

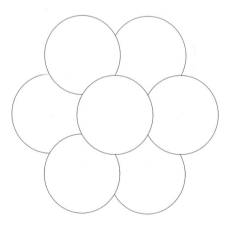

Figure 9–17. The egg of life.

Figure 9–18. The flower of life.

Figure 9–19. The seven circles in the flower of life.

Figure 9–20. The flower of life as it is usually depicted.

been shown this way traditionally because the secret societies that passed it along wanted to hide the next image, which is the "fruit of life." If you look at Figure 9–20 you will notice that there are lines and circles that just seem to end, but if you complete all the circles and continue with the rotation, you will get to the "fruit of life" (Fig. 9–21).

There is another way of getting to the fruit of life. Looking again at the flower of life, you will see seven circles that fit perfectly into one larger circle. This is an alternate method of depicting the flower of life (Fig. 9–22).

If you take one half the radius of the center circle, draw a new circle using the one half radius, and then run the circles down the three axes, you immediately get the fruit of life (Fig. 9–23). This means that the fruit of life is contained proportionally within the flower of life.

If you do this one more time (Fig. 9–24), you end up with thirteen circles connected to thirteen circles, etc.... or the fruit of life connected to the fruit of life. You can keep

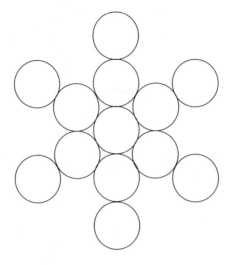

Figure 9–21. The fruit of life.

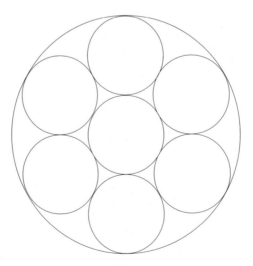

Figure 9–22. The flower of life, showing the seven circles
that fit perfectly into one larger circle.

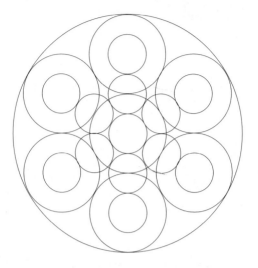

Figure 9–23. The fruit of life.

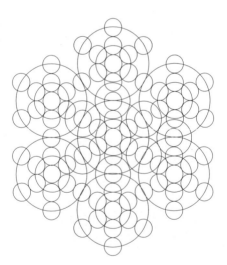

Figure 9–24. Thirteen circles connected to thirteen circles, etc.,
or the fruit of life connected to the fruit of life, etc.

repeating this operation forever—there is no beginning and no end. Like the logarithmic spiral (which we will soon discuss), this is a primary geometrical pattern of the universe.

The fruit of life is a very special, very sacred figure. It gives forth the reason for the creation. Thirteen systems of information come out of the fruit of life; we are going to go through one of them here. The full thirteen systems describe in detail every single aspect of our reality, everything that we can think of, see, sense, taste, or smell, right down to the actual atomic structure.

You get to these thirteen systems of information by combining geometric female with male energy. When male and female combine, something new is manifested. Except for the very first form, all of the shapes I have been describing have been female energy curved lines, so one of the simplest and most obvious ways of adding male energy, in straight lines, is to connect all the centers of the spheres on the fruit of life. If you do that you end up with a figure known as Metatron's Cube (Fig. 9–25).

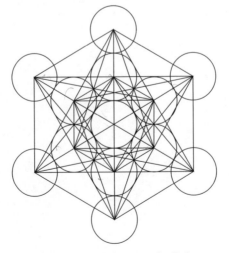

Figure 9–25. Metatron's Cube.

Metatron's Cube contains within it the five Platonic solids (Fig. 9–26). These include the cube or the hexahedron, which has six square faces, eight corners, and twelve edges; the tetrahedron, which has four triangular faces, four corners, and six edges; the octahedron, which has eight triangular faces, six corners, and twelve edges; the dodecahedron, which has twelve pentagonal faces, twenty corners, and thirty edges; and the icosahedron, which has twenty triangular faces, twelve corners, and thirty edges. The criteria for Platonic solids are that all their edges be equal, that there only be one surface and one angle, and that the points all fit on the surface of a sphere. There are only five shapes known that fit these criteria. The Platonic solids were named after Plato even though Pythagoras used them 200 years earlier; he called them the perfect solids.

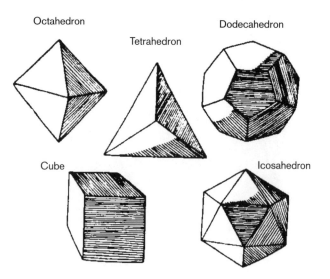

Figure 9–26. The five Platonic solids.

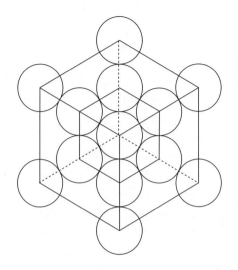

Figure 9–27. The cube extracted from Metatron's Cube.

Figure 9–28. The star tetrahedron extracted
from Metatron's Cube.

These five figures are of enormous importance. They are the components of the energy fields around our bodies. It is a little-known fact that the five Platonic solids come out of Metatron's Cube. Most of the authors of books on sacred geometry don't seem to understand or realize this fact.

To obtain the Platonic solids from Metatron's Cube you have to erase certain lines. By removing lines in a particular fashion you first of all come up with the cube shown in Figure 9–27. This is a view of the cube on end; it's a two-dimensional image of a three-dimensional object, and it contains a cube within a cube in a very specific ratio.

When you erase other lines in a prescribed way you come up with the tetrahedron shown in Figure 9–28. It is actually two tetrahedrons back-to-back, or a star tetrahedron.

Figure 9–29 shows the octahedron, which is back-to-back pyramids, and Figure 9–30 shows the icosahedron.

The dodecahedron is also contained in Metatron's Cube, but I have not yet learned how to extract it. It took Drunvalo twenty years to figure it out, so I don't feel so bad.

In the ancient schools of Egypt and Atlantis these five shapes plus the sphere were also categorized from another point of view. The ancient schools viewed the elements fire, earth, air, water, and ether as having protean shape. The shapes of the elements corresponded to the Platonic solids as follows: the tetrahedron is fire, the cube is earth, the octahedron is air, the icosahedron is water, and the dodecahedron is ether or *prana*. The sphere is the voidness from which all came. So from these six shapes all things can be created.

Atoms, the particles from which matter is formed, are simply spheres with electrons moving around their outer core at nine-tenths the speed of light. This rotation forms an electron cloud, which mimics a sphere. In crystals the different-sized atoms (spheres) align in a straight edge, a triangle, a tetrahedron, a cube, an octahedron, an icosahedron, or a dodecahedron.

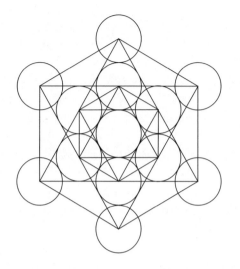

Figure 9–29. The octahedron extracted from Metatron's Cube.

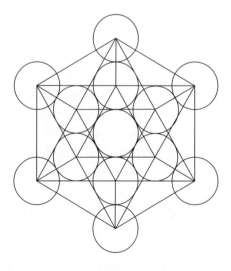

Figure 9–30. The icosahedron extracted from Metatron's Cube.

Humans

Even though it may not look like it, in fact we are nothing but geometrical images and shapes, both inside and out.

Before conception the ovum is a sphere. It is the largest cell in the human body, 200 times greater than the average cell. In fact, it is large enough to be seen with the naked eye. So the ovum is one sphere and inside is another sphere, the female pronucleus. It contains half the chromosomes for a human, twenty-two plus one. The membrane (zona pellucida) surrounding the ovum has an inner and outer thickness. In the zona pellucida are two polar bodies.

Conception begins when the sperm reaches the ovum. It takes hundreds of sperm to accomplish this. From these hundreds of sperm eleven, twelve, or thirteen work together as a unit. Through their total unified action, one of the sperm gets to enter the ovum. The sperm tail then breaks off and the head of the sperm forms a sphere exactly the same size as the female pronucleus. These then merge and form a *vesica piscis*. At that point the two merged cells contain all the knowledge of the universe.

In the next step the sperm and ovum pass right through each other and become cell number one, which is the human zygote. Now it contains forty-four plus two chromosomes. Next mitosis occurs (Fig. 9–31) and the polar bodies migrate to opposite ends of the cell and form a north and south pole. Then a tube forms seemingly out of nowhere. The chromosomes split, with half going to one side of the tube and half to the other side. The actual proportions of an adult body originate here; there is a "little person" in the original cell.

The zygote then splits into four cells and forms a tetrahedron inside a sphere (Fig. 9–32). The next division yields eight cells and a star tetrahedron, which is also a cube (Fig. 9–33). At this point it is the egg of life. The eight cells appear

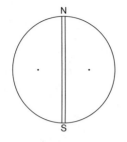

Figure 9–31. Mitosis begins.

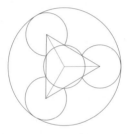

Figure 9–32. The zygote splits into four cells
and forms a tetrahedron inside a sphere.

Figure 9–33. The next division yields eight cells
and a star tetrahedron.

to be identical in all ways and are closer to who we really are than our outer package or bodies. The location of these eight cells is in the geometrical center of the body, at the base of the spine or the perineum, and they are immortal relative to our bodies. All the energy fields and grids around our bodies are centered on these eight cells. We grow radially out from there.

The first eight cells then divide into eight more cells and form a cube within a cube. That is the last time cellular division is symmetrically geometrical. When you go from sixteen to thirty-two cells there are two spaces left over, and when you go from thirty-two to sixty-four it becomes even more asymetrical. The embryo starts to become hollow and returns to the shape of a sphere. The north pole goes through the hollow ball, grows down, and connects with the south pole, forming a hollow tube in the middle and curling into a tube torus. One end becomes the mouth and the other the anus. From here widescale differentiation begins to take place. In other words, the characteristics of the particular life form, be it human, animal, insect, or whatever, begins to dominate.

This is the sequence then: Life begins as an ovum or a sphere, turns into a tetrahedron, then into a star tetrahedron, then into a cube, then into another sphere, and then into a torus.

Phi Ratio

Now let's take a look at the geometry in the space around our bodies. The first concept I want to introduce here is the phi ratio. This is a transcendental number, meaning that it never repeats itself. It is approximated at 1.6180339, but it doesn't end there; it just keeps going on literally forever. The relevance of the phi ratio is that it is found in *all* known organic structure.

The phi ratio is a proportion. If you have a line (C) and you break C into A and B in a manner that reflects this particular proportion, then A divided by B is equal to C divided by A, or 1.6180339 (Fig. 9–34).

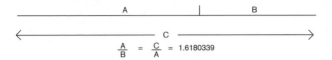

$$\frac{A}{B} = \frac{C}{A} = 1.6180339$$

Figure 9–34. Phi ratio.

We can see how the phi ratio is derived by looking at Figure 9–35. If you start with a square and then draw a line down its middle as shown in the diagram, then make a diagonal (which is line D in the diagram), and with a compass, rotate the diagonal line, then A divided by B is equal to C divided by A, and the proportion comes out to 1.6180339.

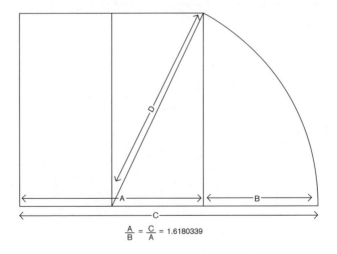

$$\frac{A}{B} = \frac{C}{A} = 1.6180339$$

Figure 9–35. How phi ratio is derived.

The bone structure of organic life is based on the phi ratio. For example, in humans the bones in the fingers all stand in phi ratios. The first bone in the finger is in phi ratio to the second, and the second to the third, etc. This is also true of the bones in the feet and the legs.

All laws are contained in your own body's proportions. The image of the fields around your body is the same image that surrounds everything and through which everything was created.

Look at Leonardo da Vinci's famous drawing, "Proportions of the Human Body" (Fig. 9–36). The arms extend straight out and the feet straight down. This forms a square

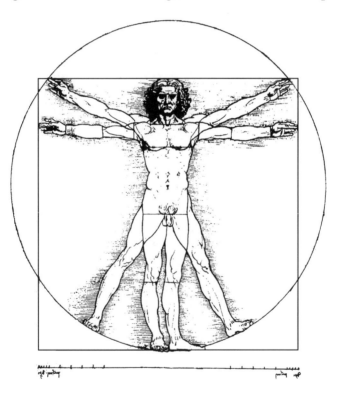

Figure 9–36. "Proportions of the Human Body."

or cube that fits around the body. Its center is at the base of the spine where the original eight cells are. Those cells also form a tiny cube there. So you have a tiny cube inside the body at the base of the spine and a bigger cube formed outside around the body.

When you spread the figure's arms and legs, a sphere or a circle forms with its center at the navel. The circle and the square meet at the feet, and the distance between the navel and the base of the spine is exactly one half the distance from the top of the head to the circle's edge. If you move the center of the circle down from the navel to the base of the spine, you get the image of the phi ratio (Fig. 9–37). The phi-ratio

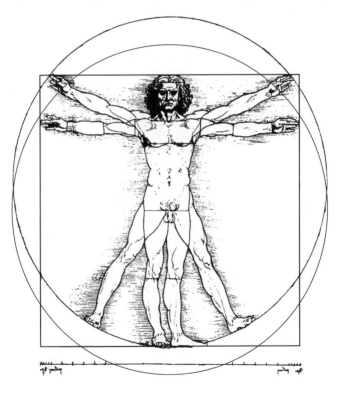

Figure 9–37. The phi ratio image.

image in this case would occur when the perimeter of the square and the circumference of the circle were equal (Fig. 9–38).

Thus you can put a square around a body with a north-south pole running down the middle, and from that you can mathematically derive the phi ratio. See Figure 9–35.

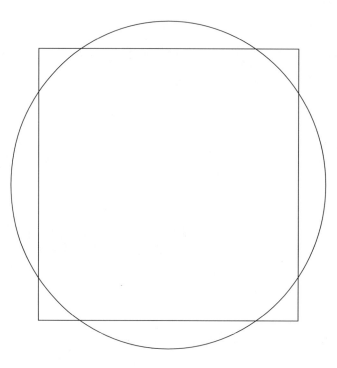

Figure 9–38. When the perimeter of the square and the circumference of the circle are equal, the phi ratio image is produced.

The Spiral

Go back to the square that fits around the body with the line running down the middle and the diagonal. Use a compass to rotate the diagonal line and complete the rectangle by extending the two remaining lines until they meet. You then have a golden mean rectangle (Fig. 9–39).

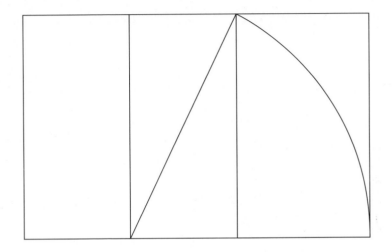

Figure 9–39. The golden mean rectangle.

The golden mean rectangle is such that if you take its shortest edge and make a square, what is left is another rectangle proportional to the bigger one by 1.618; it goes in forever and it goes out forever. This creates a spiral that goes in and out infinitely (Fig. 9–40). So the spiral is derived from the golden mean rectangle. The golden mean rectangle has two fields: male energy as the diagonal of the squares, and female energy as the curved line of the spiral.

The Fibonacci Sequence

Leonardo Fibonacci, a medieval mathematician, noticed a particular order or sequence that plant life utilizes to grow and discovered that this particular ratio kept coming up everywhere. The sequence is: 1, 1, 2, 3, 5, 8, 13, 21, 34, 55, 89, 144, 233, etc. I referred to it earlier when discussing the growth of a plant.

The reason this pattern shows up consistently in life originates in the golden mean spiral which goes in and out for-

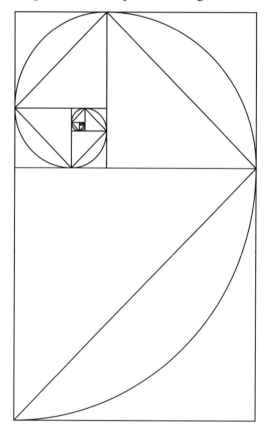

Figure 9–40. Spiral—golden mean rectangle.

ever, without beginning or end. Life doesn't know how to deal with something that has no beginning because there is nowhere to start. So this sequence, which has become known as the Fibonacci sequence, is life's solution to that problem.

If you divide one term of this sequence into the next one and keep going, you will find that you quickly approximate the transcendental number 1.6180339.

For example:

1 divided by 1 = 1
2 divided by 1 = 2
3 divided by 2 = 1.5
5 divided by 3 = 1.66
8 divided by 5 = 1.60
13 divided by 8 = 1.625
21 divided by 13 = 1.615
34 divided by 21 = 1.619
55 divided by 34 = 1.617
89 divided by 55 = 1.6181

From this you can see that you keep going from under to over the transcendental number 1.6180339 sequentially. You keep getting closer and closer to the exact phi ratio of 1.6180339 without ever actually attaining it. However, you very quickly get so close that you cannot tell the difference. This is life's way of dealing with something that has no beginning and no end.

Figure 9–41 shows how it works geometrically. Use the diagonal of the first square as your measuring unit, move one unit; then make a 90-degree turn and move one more unit; then turn 90 degrees and move two diagonals; then turn another 90 degrees and move three diagonals; then 90 degrees and five, then 90 degrees and eight, etc. . . . The spiral is unfolding exactly as in nature.

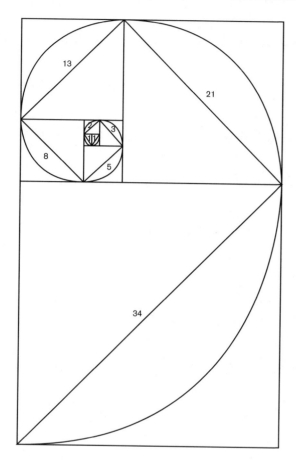

Figure 9–41. Fibonacci spiral.

Figure 9–42 depicts the geometrical comparison between a logarithmic golden mean rectangle on the bottom and a Fibonacci rectangle on the top. A Fibonacci rectangle is just six equal squares. It also has a definite beginning as compared to the logarithmic golden mean rectangle, which goes in forever. As you can see, they approximate each other very quickly.

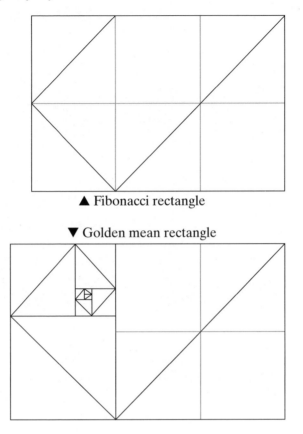

▲ Fibonacci rectangle

▼ Golden mean rectangle

Figure 9–42. Golden mean rectangle versus Fibonacci rectangle.

Going back to da Vinci's sketch, we note that he drew lines on the body—on the arms in various places, on the knees, in the center, and in the chest, neck, etc.... If you extend these lines you will create an eight-by-eight grid or sixty-four squares (Fig. 9–43).

The eight spirals of energy around the human body are based on the Fibonacci sequence. These spirals of energy come in and focus in the eight squares that surround the four central squares. See Figure 9–44.

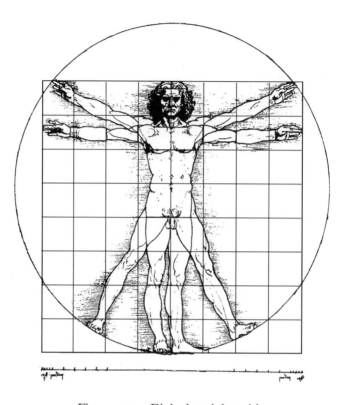

Figure 9–43. Eight-by-eight grid.

Figure 9–45 shows the sixty-four squares with the spirals of energy. The spirals come in two different ways. Figure 9–46 shows one way. The starting points are the eight squares that surround the four center squares. You can trace any of these spirals using the Fibonacci sequence of 1, 1, 2, 3, 5, 8, 13, etc. These are called "white light spirals." They are male, and their primary medium is electrical.

The spirals can also go the other way, as shown in Figure 9–47. If you form them this way, you have to go through the center zero point; this is the womb or void. These are called

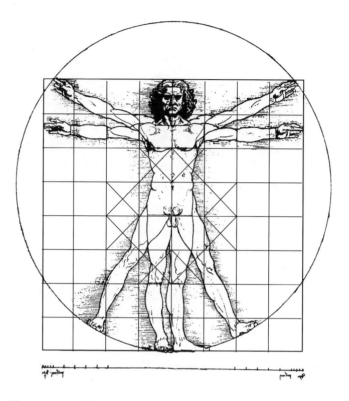

Figure 9–44. The spirals of energy focus in the eight squares
that surround the four center squares.

"black light spirals." They are female, and their primary medium is magnetic.

You could also superimpose the original eight cells of the
human zygote, or the "egg of life," over this grid. This geometry is true for us from conception through adulthood.

The Chakra Systems

The harmonics of music and our body's chakra system are
related in the geometrical pattern called the "egg of life." As

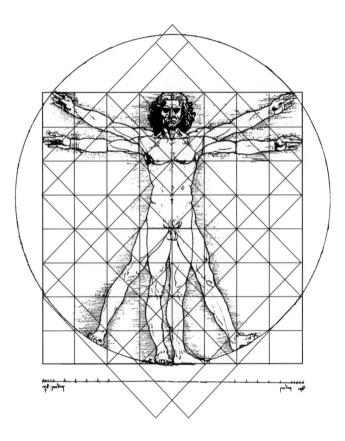

Figure 9–45. The spirals of energy.

shown on Figure 9–48, between the third and fourth and the
seventh and eighth notes of the musical scale, there are half
steps. No one seems to know why. Some people also describe
a break or change between the fourth and fifth notes. There
is a reflection pattern. One, two, three, half step, four; one,
two, three, half step, four—there are really two sets of four.
One is female and one is male.

The reason there are half steps between the third and
fourth notes and the seventh and eighth notes, and a break

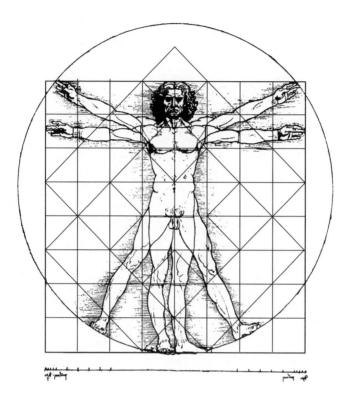

Figure 9–46. "White light spirals"; they are male,
their primary nature is electrical.

between the fourth and fifth notes, is that sound can be explained in terms of the egg of life (Fig. 9–49). As sound comes in from below it hits sphere number one. From there it has three other places to go on this tetrahedron—from sphere number one to number two, then to number three; it moves in a triangle—a flat plane in the same direction. Then, in order for the sound wave to move to the fourth sphere, it has to change direction. The fourth sphere is directly behind sphere number five. Because the sound wave changes direc-

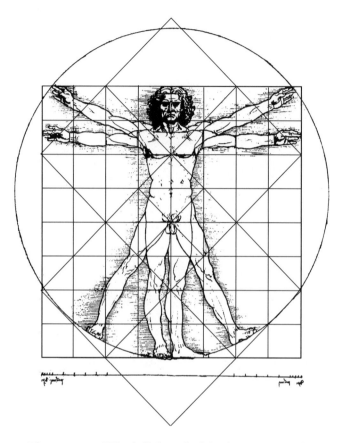

Figure 9–47. "Black light spirals"; they are female,
their primary nature is magnetic.

tion it is perceived as traveling a shorter distance, hence the
half step, just as the shadow of a line appears to shorten as
it changes direction. The sound wave has now completed
the first tetrahedron and goes into the second tetrahedron.
To do this it must go through the voidness in the center of
the egg of life, the Great Void, to get to sphere number five.
Sound changes polarity when it moves to the second tetrahedron, from male to female or from female to male. It then

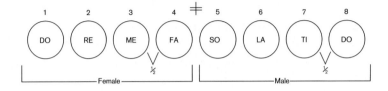

Figure 9–48. The harmonics of music.

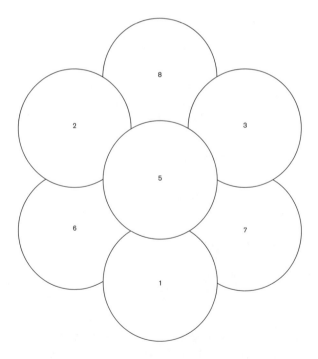

Figure 9–49. How sound is related to the egg of life.

moves to spheres number six and seven in a flat plane, where it must make another half step to go to sphere number eight.

The eight-point chakra system described by Drunvalo resembles the movement of the eight notes on the musical scale; however, in the chakra system of the human body the "egg of life pattern" is unfolded. The chakras start at the base of the spine and move up over the head (Fig. 9–50). This,

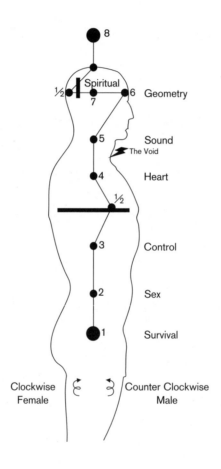

Figure 9–50. The eight-point chakra system.

according to Drunvalo, is a Hindu or Tibetan system and is greatly simplified. Drunvalo says that we also have chakra systems above and below our bodies. The one below our feet is the consciousness level from which we came, and the one above our head is the next level, the consciousness toward which we are moving. They are in phi ratio. The one below is very short and the one above is very long.

The same half steps that we observed in the musical scale also recur in the chakra system. The chakras are like lenses though which we interpret reality. For example, when a new spirit is born its total concern is with survival—being able to stay here on this third-dimensional level. The next thing the spirit wants to do is make physical contact with other beings. Contact is first made with the mother, later it becomes sexual. Once you have established yourself and made sexual contact, establishing control follows. These represent the first three chakras from the bottom up; then there is a big wall and a half step change of direction. You can't get through this wall until you have mastered these three chakras. Once you do get through you are at the heart, which is the fourth chakra in this system. The fifth is located at the throat and is related to music; the sixth, between the eyes, is related to geometry, and the seventh, located at the pineal gland, is the "third eye." At this point there is another wall with another half-step change of direction. This takes us to the eighth chakra, which is above the head and points to our next phase in our conscious evolution.

This eight-point system represents only the white notes of the musical scale and, as I mentioned, Drunvalo said it was a greatly simplified system. There are five black notes, or sharps and flats, to the musical scale as well. So there are really twelve chakra points, with the one above the head being the thirteenth (Fig. 9–51). The twelve represent five

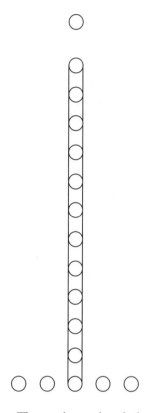

Figure 9–51. The twelve-point chakra system.

subchakras at each site, so there are actually sixty points. Each of the twelve groups of five is separated by 90 degrees.

A straight tube runs through the body, perfectly straight like a fluorescent bulb, starting at the perineum at the base of the spine and continuing up through the soft spot in the head. The twelve chakra points fall along this line at an average of 7.23 centimeters between each of the twelve points and the next, or the distance across the palms of the average hand, likewise the distance from the tip of your chin to the tip of your nose.

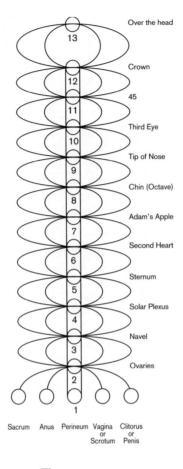

Figure 9–52.

Energy spirals up through the chakra system making 90-degree turns as it moves from one chakra point to the next. At the base chakra (Fig. 9–52) all five channels are pointing frontwards in a straight line. The opening to the vagina is a *vesica piscis* and the small opening in the penis is also a *vesica piscis.* All the energy in these five points flows from front to back. As the energy moves up 7.23 centimeters to the second chakra and the ovaries it shifts direction by 90 degrees.

Up another 7.23 centimeters (with another 90-degree shift) is the navel. This is where the umbilical cord was attached. The energy here moves from back to front, the reverse of the base chakra. When we move up again to the solar plexus, which is another *vesica piscis,* the energy radiates out from side to side again as in the ovaries. The next level is the sternum, which is a special point affiliated with the circle (Fig. 9–53). The fifth chakra is the first instance of return; it is special because it contains all the previous motions at once. The energy has made a complete 360-degree rotation and knows all the directions. Hence you have the breasts coming out to the front but also being separated sideways. This is the Christ-consciousness point. It is at the 19.5 degree latitude of the body and it forms a cross. At the sixth point you have the

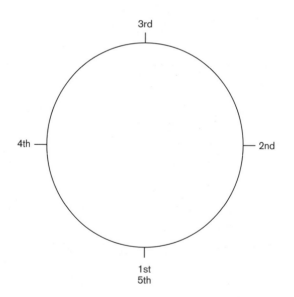

Figure 9–53. The fifth chakra—the sternum.
The energy has made a complete 360-degree rotation
and knows all the directions.

heart; at the seventh is the Adam's apple; the eighth is the chin. Then you hit another octave and the energy runs through the head. The physical features of the face that correspond to the chakra points in the head begin with the chin. From the chin the energy rotates 90 degrees to the mouth (energy running side to side), then to the nose (energy moving back to front), then to the eyes (side to side energy), and then to the third eye where the energy has again made a 360-degree rotation.

The External Chakra Points

We have external chakra points too, points in the space around our bodies. We are surrounded by shape in the form of a star tetrahedron with eight external chakra points on it (Fig. 9–54). If you were to photograph the internal points they would be identical to the external ones. All the external points pulse in unison just like the internal ones. We thus have both an internal and an external aspect to our chakra systems.

In the components of the star tetrahedron around our bodies, the tetrahedron pointing up toward the sky is male, and the tetrahedron pointing down toward the Earth is female (Fig. 9–54). This is true for both men and women. There are only two ways that a person can symmetrically fit into the star tetrahedron. If the point at the base of the male tetrahedron is forward, the male fits, and if the point at the base of the female tetrahedron is forward, the female fits. The star tetrahedron is linked to the center of the body at the base of the spine. If you jump the external star tetrahedron goes up with you, and if you sit it moves down with you.

Figure 9–54 shows two-dimensionally how the male fits into the star tetrahedron. If this drawing represented a female she would be facing backwards. Figure 9–55 gives a top view of how a male and female would fit into the star tetrahedron.

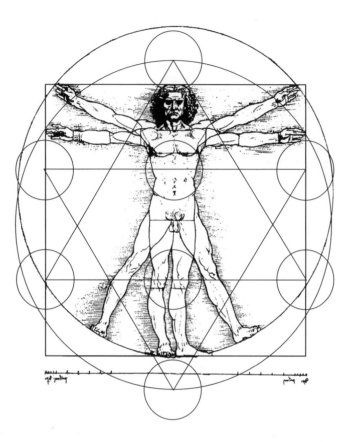

Figure 9–54. Our external chakra points.

The Eye

Drunvalo has drawn the morphogenic structure of the eye, be it human or the eye of any other creature. He considers it to be his most important representation (Fig. 9–56). The ocular structure is the same as the structure of light itself; it contains the entire electromagnetic structure. This structure also contains the geometry of the *vesica piscis*. Within the *vesica piscis* are two equilateral triangles. The concurrent

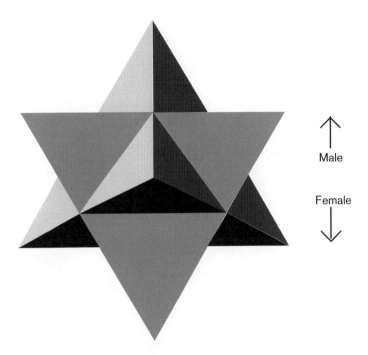

Male

Female

Figure 9–55. A top view of how males and females
fit into the star tetrahedron.

base of the triangles is the width of the *vesica piscis,* and the
line running through their center is its length. When you
rotate the length of the first *vesica piscis* 90 degrees it becomes
the width of the next larger *vesica piscis.* If you rotate this
vesica piscis another 90 degrees its length will become the
width of the next larger one, and so on. This goes in forever
and it goes out forever.

An electromagnetic field, or light, is an electric field with
a magnetic field moving at 90 degrees to it (Fig. 9–57). The
electrical field is moving in a wave and the magnetic field is
moving at 90 degrees to this wave, and the whole configura-
tion is rotating as it moves through space (Fig. 9–58).

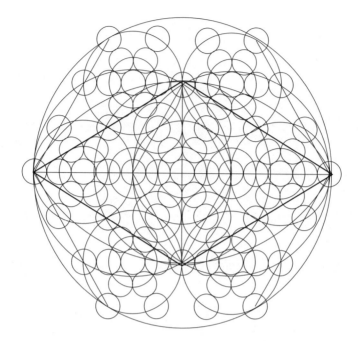

Figure 9–56. The morphogenic structure of all eyes.

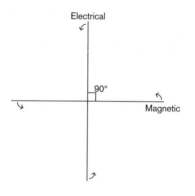

Figure 9–57. An electromagnetic field.

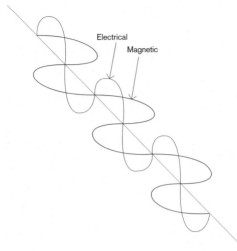

Figure 9–58. An electromagnetic field.

Drunvalo predicts that scientists will discover, in any electromagnetic field, that the electrical aspect is the length of the first *vesica piscis* and the magnetic aspect is the width of the first *vesica piscis,* and these are in proportion to each other. They rotate by 90 degrees as they spiral out, just like the *vesica piscis.* Logarithmic spirals also move along electromagnetic spirals of energy. The light field itself and the eye that receives it are in the same geometric pattern because the receiver has to tune to that which it is receiving. Our whole bodies are tuned to sound, vibration, music, and light.

Notes

1. Stan Tenen, "Geometric Metaphors of Life," 108–minute videotape (1990). The MERU Foundation, P.O. Box 1738, San Anselmo, CA 94979.

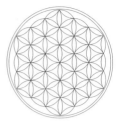

10

The Left Eye of Horus

The "Left Eye of Horus" was a twelve-year "emotional body" training for aspiring Egyptian initiates. It dealt with various emotions, feelings, fears, and both positive and negative aspects of the chakras. All the temples in Egypt were built for "Left Eye of Horus" trainings. In this course, initiates worked with many different aspects of human nature. There is a specific fear related to each of the chakras, and each of the twelve major temples in Egypt dealt with the fear related to a specific chakra.

In the temple that dealt with fears associated with the second chakra, according to Drunvalo, there is a huge hole in the ground (Fig. 10–1). Even modern Egyptian guides tell tourists this hole was part of a training process for the initiates who studied there. An initiate had to go into this hole, and the hole was filled with water. Huge stones were placed in the hole, and they had to be careful not to hit them. The training included getting to the bottom of the hole, passing through a small opening, and then coming out the other side.

It doesn't seem so difficult, but this is not the full story of what the initiates were doing here. Egyptologists know from ancient writings merely that there was water in the hole and that it was part of a training, but they really do not know

Figure 10–1. The hole in the ground.

what the particulars were. Drunvalo asked Thoth for an explanation as to the real initiation, and Thoth gave him the following account:

The temple complex was situated such that the initiation began on a much higher level than the hole in the ground. The initiation was set up so that the students could see only three steps leading into water at the beginning, and then a very high wall on the other side of the water (Fig. 10–2). The initiates had to go down the three steps and into the water, and then in one breath come out but not the same way. They had to work their way slowly because it was dark and also because there were obstacles. So they swam all the way down to the bottom of the hole; there they found a passageway leading to a huge tank. This tank was lit up so they could see it, and it was filled with crocodiles. At this point the initiates could see an opening at the top of the tank. What they would almost always do, according to Thoth, was head past the crocodiles and go straight for the opening.

The only problem was if they did this they failed, meaning they had to go again. The second time the initiate knew two things: they knew the opening they saw was not the correct way out, and they knew that the tank was filled with crocodiles. Having seen the crocodiles in the flesh probably

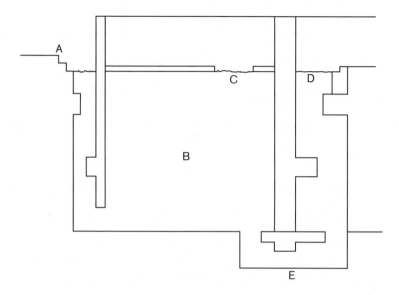

Figure 10–2. Left Eye of Horus training. A—the initiate begins here, B—tank filled with crocodiles, C—the incorrect exit, D—the correct exit, E—the Figure 10–1 hole in the ground.

made it much more fearsome when they had to repeat the test. At the moment of their greatest terror, then, they had to go even deeper into the tank of crocodiles and out the other side.

The Great Pyramid

After twelve years of the Left Eye of Horus training (the emotional body training) and twelve more years of the Right Eye of Horus training (the unity consciousness training), the Egyptian student would descend into the Great Pyramid for a three-and-a-half-day period of final initiation.

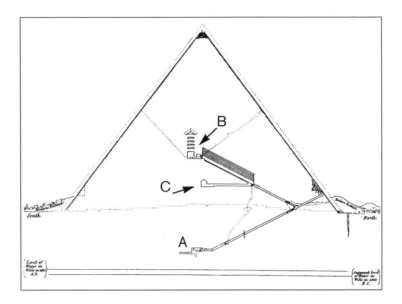

Figure 10–3. Initiation in the Great Pyramid. The initiation
began underneath the Great Pyramid (A). Then it moved to the
King's chamber (B) and finally to the Queen's chamber (C).

   Thoth says that the pyramids were built specifically to
bring someone from the second level of consciousness (where
we are presently) into the third level, which is Christ-consciousness. The Great Pyramid is an initiation chamber.
   The King's and Queen's chambers in the Great Pyramid
were given these names by the Muslims because of the sug-
gestive design of these chambers. The roof of the King's
chamber is flat, and Muslims buried their men under flat
roofs. The Queen's chamber has a pitched roof and the Muslims buried their women under like roofs. According to Drunvalo, these chambers had nothing to do with burials—they
were initiation chambers, period.

The initiation didn't begin inside the Great Pyramid. It began underneath it. From under the Great Pyramid the initiation moved to the King's chamber and finally the Queen's chamber (Fig. 10–3). The process began in a room under the Great Pyramid because the initiates needed first to encounter the "black light" spiral which goes into the center of the Earth as well as into the Halls of Amenti. Such a tunnel still exists underneath the Great Pyramid and seems to end in the middle of nowhere. No one today seems to know why.

According to Drunvalo, the tunnel is located where it is in order to connect to the "black light spiral" at the soonest possible point after the spiral has passed through zero point or the Great Void. This tunnel is in fact a "black light spiral" initiation chamber. Whatever you think in that tunnel becomes real because it is a true fourth-dimensional space. Many people have died here because they manifested their fears. So many unusual things have happened in this tunnel that in recent years the Egyptian government has blocked it off from tourists. Good idea—tourists do not usually know what to do when they find themselves in the fourth dimension.

In this tunnel is the first phase of initiation into Christ-consciousness, which itself is primarily a totally different way of interpreting reality. From there the initiation moves to the King's chamber. The King's chamber is designed to catch the "white light" spiral at its source, and to filter out the "black light" one. The King's chamber seems to be off-center but the sarcophagus in the chamber is placed in such a way that, if you are lying in it, the "white light" spiral goes directly through your pineal gland. The initiates would recline in the sarcophagus for three and a half days, leave the third-dimensional world, and experience incredible consciousness expansion. They could then find their way back to their bodies because they were using principles of the Fibonacci spiral and not the golden-mean logarithmic spiral. As I discussed earlier, the logarithmic spiral has no beginning and no end, but the Fibonacci spiral does have a definite beginning. The initiates could trace their way back into their bodies because they had one point of reference on the Fibonacci spiral.

After this mind-boggling transformation of self and reality, the initiate then went to the Queen's chamber, which serves as a stabilizing room. Once a person has gone through the experience in the King's chamber successfully, he or she is altered dramatically and needs some settling. This is what the Queen's chamber was, a sanctuary for stabilizing Christ-consciousness.

When archaeologists first opened the sarcophagus in the King's chamber, they found an unusual white crystalline powder which they scooped up to examine. The powder is now in the British Museum. No one knew what it was until recently, and the explanation is the last thing anyone expected. Scientists have since found that when you are in a particular deep state of meditation you excrete a certain chemical from your pituitary gland, which crystallizes into a powder. There was quite a lot of this powder found in the sarcophagus in the King's chamber, indicating that there must have been many people initiated there.

Many people have theorized that the Great Pyramid was a burial place. However, there is a lot of evidence to suggest that it was not a burial place at all, but was in fact a place of initiation. Without exception, in every case in ancient Egypt that a person of prominence died, the priests cut out the heart and various organs and placed them into four jars. They mummified the person, put the body into a sarcophagus, placed the lid on, and sealed it. The body was then carried to a burial place. The sarcophagus in the King's chamber is bigger than the doorway. This means it had to have been put in there while the place was being built, not the custom for burials at all.

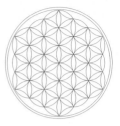

11

The Hall of Records

According to Edgar Cayce, the famous psychic, the opening
to the Hall of Records, which holds the history of the Earth,
will be found in the right paw of the Sphinx. This has been
clearly marked geometrically. Looking at Figure 11–1, if you
bisect the golden mean rectangle that fits around the spiral
at the Giza plateau, it passes exactly through the headdress
of the Sphinx. Also, a line extended from the southern face
of the middle pyramid and the line that bisects the golden
mean rectangle form a cross that marks a very specific spot
on the right shoulder of the Sphinx.

The Sphinx is now under major renovation, and one of
the problems with it is that the right shoulder—the area
marked by the cross—keeps breaking open. The Egyptians
have been trying to patch it to keep it together. The head is
also falling off. About six or seven years ago, Thoth told
Drunvalo that the head will fall off and that, in the neck,
there will be found a large golden sphere, which is a time
capsule. The Egyptians are doing everything they can to keep
the head and right shoulder from falling off.

Thoth says everything was set up at a higher level so that
the Hall of Records would be discovered before the end of
1990. Drunvalo is not sure if it has happened or not. Thoth

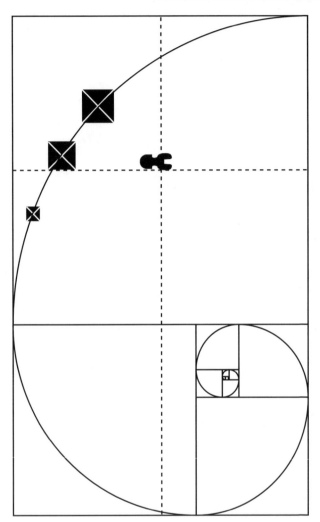

Figure 11–1. The opening to the Hall of Records is
geometrically marked in the right shoulder of the Sphinx.

said 148 sets of three people would try to enter the Hall of
Records, until one of these sets, coming from the West, would
open the doorway by making a sound with their voice. Inside

there would be a spiral staircase going into an underground room. The Japanese have the technical ability to see this room clearly enough with instruments to detect a clay pot in the corner.

There are three channels that go out from this room. If you know how to read it, the clay pot will tell you where to go and what to do. Thoth said that the three people from the West would enter and go down the right channel. If you go down the wrong channel, or if you are not the right group of people, you will die—a real "Indiana Jones"-type scene.

If you are one of the chosen three people you can walk right in without any problem. These three people eventually will come down a long stone hallway lit on its own with no lights; that is, the air itself would be luminous. High up on the left side of the wall would be etched forty-eight sacred geometry drawings. These are the illustrations of the chromosomes of Christ-consciousness, the first one being the flower of life. At the end of the hallway there is a slight right-hand turn into a large room. Sitting on the raised shelves of this room is physical evidence of the existence of civilization on this planet for the last 5½ million years. At the front of the room is a stone. At the top of the stone these three people would find something like a photograph, an image of themselves. Beneath the images in the photograph they would find their names—not necessarily the names they were given at birth, but their true names. Underneath the names would be a date, which would be that actual day. Originally Thoth was going to meet these three people but he is now gone. Unless it happened before May 4, 1991, someone else will meet them. Thoth said that each of these three people will be allowed to remove one of these objects and take it out.

The Hall of Records contains more than physical objects. Under the Sphinx, in the Hall of Records, information is stored on many different dimensional levels.

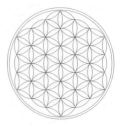

12

Prana

When the poles last shifted in 10,500 B.C. and we fell in con-sciousness, Drunvalo says we stopped breathing in the ancient way that we had practiced for so long. We started breathing in the way that we do now, which is very unusual. Hardly anyone else in our universe breathes this way.

In general, there are two things which we take in when we breathe. There is air and there is prana. Prana is life-force energy itself, more vital than air for our existence. Prana is not just in the air, it is everywhere. There is nowhere that it is not; it even exists in a vacuum or a void.

Prana exists as an energy field connected so closely with spirit that spirit cannot exist without it. If you take air away you have a couple of minutes before you die; if you take water away you have even more time; and if you take food away you have more time still, but if you break prana from spirit, death is instantaneous. So taking in prana with breath is a crucial act in sustaining our form of life.

We are supposed to breathe such that while air comes in through our mouth and nose, we take the prana in through the top of our heads—that is, what once was the soft spot on the top of our heads. Simultaneously, we take the prana in from below through the perineum. The prana channel through the body is about two inches in diameter and extends one hand length above the head and one hand length below the feet. It connects with the crystalline grid around the body. The prana then comes from above and below the body and meets in one of the chakras. The chakra in which the prana meets depends on where you are mentally, emotionally, and dimensionally "tuned." This is a very specific science.

After the poles shifted we stopped breathing in this manner and started taking in the prana through our mouth and nose directly with the air. The prana then bypassed the pineal gland in the center of the head. The pineal gland is an eye, the third eye, not the pituitary gland. It is shaped like an eyeball, round, hollow, and with a lens for focusing light and color receptors. It is designed to receive light from above to go to every cell in the body instantaneously. As it is shaped like an eye it is also a *vesica piscis,* the image which comes out of the first day of Genesis. This geometrical shape is the beginning of all creation, and contained within it is all sacred information of the universe.

When the pineal gland is not activated, however, it turns off. Normally this gland should be about the size of a quarter but in us it has become the size of a pea because we haven't used it for about 13,000 years. The direct result of turning off the pineal gland is polarity consciousness—good and bad, right and wrong.

Because of the way we breathe we see things in terms of good and evil, but in fact there is no such thing as polarity. Everything actually has three components—the holy trinity—and no matter what polarity you think of there will be a third element to it; for example, with hot and cold, there is warm, up and down gives you middle, etc. From higher dimensional levels of existence polarity is just an illusion. Unity is all there is; there is just one God and one Spirit that moves through everything. All that ever occurs then is occurring because of the one God.

On our level of existence we interpret things differently. We think we see good and evil. What is really going on, however, is timing. The forces of polarity are necessary for the proper functioning of the universe. Remember, the dark forces do everything they can to hinder a particular area of consciousness, be it on a planetary or individual scale. The light forces do everything they can to encourage consciousness expansion and awareness. This opposition causes consciousness to move upward at exactly the right pace. In the birth of a child, for example, nine months is the proper time, not three months or fifteen months. The forces of polarity cause the child to be born at exactly the right time.

So given where we are, we need to see good and evil and be aware of them, but we also need to recognize that the presence of God is in every situation and that there is a reason for everything that happens. We need to see that everything is whole and complete and perfect and that there is nothing wrong no matter how bad or how good it may seem. We need to see that life engenders a deep conscious aspect that is everywhere.

In our state we tend to think that we live inside this body, that everything "out there" is separate from us, and that our feelings and thoughts don't manifest beyond ourselves. We think that we can hide our thoughts and feelings and they have no impact "out there." This is simply not true. Everything that we think, feel, and do is creating our whole world all the way out to the most distant stars. We are creating everything in every moment, more so than we could ever imagine.

Christ-Consciousness Spherical Breathing

Drunvalo teaches a meditation designed to get us back to breathing the way we did before the last pole shift. It involves taking prana in through the top of the head and also through the perineum so that energy comes from above and below the body. The prana then connects with the crystalline grid around the body (the star tetrahedron inscribed in a sphere) and meets in one of the chakras.

This breathing meditation was given to Drunvalo by the angels, which he states are really just a higher aspect of himself. He did not receive this information from Thoth.

In order to stay alive in the same body for 52,000 years, Thoth had to spend one hour a day with his head to the north and his feet to the south, centered in a chosen chakra and breathing in a certain way. He then had to turn around and reverse his polarity and spend another hour breathing.

In addition to spending two hours every day breathing consciously, Thoth had to stand in front of the "flower of life" once every fifty years. Needless to say, he was overjoyed when Drunvalo gave him this breathing meditation because then he no longer needed to do his lengthy meditations.

According to Drunvalo, the first six breaths of his spherical breathing meditation are better and more accurately balanced than Thoth's two hours of daily breathing. This "Christ-consciousness" spherical breathing is also exactly the way that whales and dolphins breathe.

The meditation is done in a series of fourteen breaths. The first six breaths are for balancing the polarities within the chakras and also for cleansing these electrical circuits. The next seven breaths reestablish the proper pranic flow through the body and recreate spherical breathing within the body. The fourteenth breath changes the balance of pranic energy within the body from third-dimensional to fourth-dimensional awareness.

This meditation is much more than just breathing, however. It uses a combination of mind, body, breath, and heart, all working together in harmony.

These breaths are the first fourteen in a series of seventeen used to create the counter-rotating fields of the merkaba around the body. Because the internal merkaba can only be created with the emotional body intact, it is absolutely necessary to open your heart and feel love and unity for all life while doing this meditation. You do this to the best of your ability, of course.

You begin by sitting in a comfortable, relaxed position with your spine straight. Close your eyes and let the outside world go. When you feel calm and relaxed, expand your feelings to a state of love and unity for all life everywhere, and also visualize the star tetrahedron around your body.

On the inhale of the first breath, visualize the male tetrahedron. This is the one with the apex facing up. The point at the base of the tetrahedron, which is just above the knees when you are standing, is facing toward the front for males and toward the back for females. Visualize to the best of your ability this male tetrahedron filled with brilliant white light. Your body is surrounded by this light.

Also on this first breath arrange your hands, palms up, with the thumb and index finger lightly touching. This is a *mudra*. Do not allow any of your other fingers to touch one another.

Inhale through your nose in a deep, relaxed, rhythmic manner for approximately seven seconds, bringing the breath up from the stomach, then to the diaphragm, and finally to the chest. Do this all in one movement.

Then without pausing at the top of the inhale, begin your exhale. Exhale slowly through your nose for approximately seven seconds. As you exhale, visualize the female tetrahedron. This is the one with the apex facing down, the point at the level of the solar plexus facing the back for males, and the front for females. Again visualize this tetrahedron filled with brilliant white light.

After you have completed the exhale in approximately seven seconds, relax and hold your breath for approximately five seconds. Move your eyes toward each other (look slightly cross-eyed, in other words), then look up and immediately look down to the ground as fast as you can. At the same time visualize the white light in the female tetrahedron shooting out through the apex of the tetrahedron and into the Earth.

As you are doing this, you should feel an electrical sensation moving down your spine. Drunvalo calls this pulsing. What you are doing is clearing out the negativity in the part of your electrical system that is associated with the mudra you used (index fingers and thumbs touching).

Immediately after pulsing the energy down your spine, begin the second breath. The second breath is exactly the same as the first breath except for one thing. The one and only change is that a different mudra is used. For the second breath you hold the thumbs and second fingers together. Everything else is the same as the first breath. Similarly, for breaths three through six, everything in these breaths is the same as the first breath except for the mudras.

For the third-breath mudra, you hold the thumb and third finger (ring finger) together. For the fourth-breath mudra, hold the thumb and little finger together. For the fifth-breath mudra, hold the thumb and index finger together just as in the first breath. And for the sixth-breath mudra, hold the thumb and second finger together, just as in the second breath.

The next seven breaths begin a different breathing pattern. It is no longer necessary to visualize the male tetrahedron on the inhale and the female tetrahedron on the exhale. What you visualize instead is the tube that runs through the body. This tube extends one hand length above the head and one hand length below the feet. In other words, the tube runs through the apex of the male tetrahedron, which extends one hand length above your head. It also runs through the apex of the female tetrahedron, extending one hand length below your feet. The diameter of your tube is exactly the same as the diameter of the hole formed when your thumb and middle finger are touching.

Begin the seventh inhale immediately after the pulse following the sixth exhale. Inhale rhythmically, taking about seven seconds, just as you inhaled for the first six breaths. As you begin the seventh inhale, visualize the tube running through your body as well as brilliant white light running up and down the tube at the same time. In other words, visualize prana, running down the tube from over your head and simultaneously running up the tube from beneath your feet.

At some point, you instantly do have brilliant white light running up and down your tube. Now visualize the light meeting inside the tube at the level of the navel or third chakra. As the two beams of light or prana meet, a sphere of light or prana about the size of a grapefruit forms and slowly begins to grow.

This all happens in the instant you begin the seventh inhale. As you continue to inhale for approximately seven seconds, the sphere of prana slowly grows. At the end of the seventh inhale, immediately begin your exhale. There is no more holding of the breath and no more pulsing.

For the next seven breaths use the same mudra, that is, both the index and second fingers lightly touching the thumb with the palms up.

As you begin to exhale, the prana continues flowing from each end of the tube and expanding the sphere centered at the navel. By the time of the full exhale (approximately seven seconds), the sphere of prana will be about eight or nine inches in diameter.

Begin the eighth breath immediately after the seventh exhale. On the eighth breath the prana sphere continues to grow until it reaches its maximum size at the end of the exhale. At its maximum the sphere is roughly the size of a volleyball.

On the ninth breath, the sphere cannot grow bigger, so what it does is grow brighter. Visualize the sphere growing brighter and brighter on both the inhale and exhale.

On the tenth breath, continue to visualize the sphere growing brighter. About halfway through the inhale, the sphere will reach critical mass and ignite into a sun. As you begin to exhale, make a small hole with your lips and blow the air out your mouth like you are forcing it out. Then let it all go with a final *whoosh*. As you do, the ignited sun expands outward to form a sphere around your body. This is the same sphere shown in Leonardo da Vinci's drawing. Your whole body is now inside a sphere of charged white light or prana.

The sphere is not yet stable at this point, however. It took all your energy just to get it out there. It will take three more breaths to stabilize it.

The eleventh, twelfth, and thirteenth breaths are needed to stabilize the sphere. Inhale and exhale just as you did for the seventh through ninth breaths, all the while feeling the flow of prana through the tube, meeting at the navel, and expanding into the sphere around your body.

The sphere is now stabilized and you are ready for the all-important fourteenth breath. For the seventh through the thirteenth breaths, the prana flow met in the tube behind the navel. That tuned us to our third-dimensional reality. If we were going to stay here we would stop after thirteen breaths. Since we are moving to the fourth dimension, the fourteenth breath becomes necessary in order to retune us to that reality.

At the beginning of the inhale of the fourteenth breath, you move the point where the two streams of prana meet up from the navel to the sternum. The entire large sphere around your body moves up as the original small sphere, which is also still contained within the large sphere, rises to the sternum. Having the prana meet here tunes you to fourth-dimensional or Christ-consciousness.

As you do this you change the mudra also. Males place the left palm on top of the right palm with the thumbs lightly touching; females place the right palm on top of the left palm with the thumbs lightly touching. Keep this mudra for the remainder of the meditation.

As you continue to breathe from your Christ-consciousness center, switch to shallow, relaxed breathing and let yourself feel the flow of prana and love for as long as you like. Drunvalo recommends spending at least ten minutes in this meditation.

It is very important to hold pure thoughts like love, truth, beauty, trust, harmony, and peace. The reason is that in the fourth dimension, or Christ-consciousness, thoughts are instantly manifested into reality. As you continue to do this meditation, your awareness increasingly tunes to fourth-dimensional consciousness. As this is happening you also become increasingly aware of the power of your thoughts and how they are unerringly creating your reality. Your thoughts then begin to manifest into reality more and more quickly, hence the importance of holding absolutely pure thoughts.

If you choose to do this meditation, it is best to practice it daily until you have become a conscious breather, that is, remembering on every breath your intimate and inseparable connection to the One Spirit that moves through everything. It is only necessary to do the fourteen breaths once a day. From there you can remember to breathe through your tube and recreate your sphere at any time throughout the day.

This sphere of prana also forms a very powerful field of

protection around you, second only to the merkaba. Your sense of safety and trust will increase as a result.

It is important in this meditation to visualize clearly the male tetrahedron on the inhale and the female tetrahedron on the exhale of the first six breaths (this is true for both men and women), each filled with brilliant white light or prana. I found it extremely useful to construct a model so I could actually step inside each tetrahedron and see how I fit into it.

I always had more trouble visualizing the male tetrahedron. I had a tendency to get confused on just where the points were at the base. I solved that by creating a model out of tent poles and string. I placed the tent poles on the floor in the shape of an equilateral triangle to form the base of the tetrahedron. I then taped string to the three corners of the triangle and held them up over my head to form the apex of the tetrahedron. The lengths of all sides of the tetrahedron are equal to your height, or equal to the length of your outspread arms. That helped me form a clear visual sense of the male tetrahedron, and as a result, improved the quality of the meditation dramatically.

I also find it helpful to trace the images of the tetrahedrons with my hands before I begin the meditation and while I am doing the first six breaths. In other words, I begin by tracing the male tetrahedron, first the base and then the sides, up to the point over my head. That seems to lock the image in place for me. I will also trace the base of the female tetrahedron at my solar plexus. I then visualize the point of the base behind my back and the sides going down until they form the apex in the ground.

It is necessary to know clearly your relationship to the star tetrahedron as you are standing or sitting. The apex of the male tetrahedron is always one hand length over your head, whether you are standing or sitting. Remember, if you are standing, the base of the male tetrahedron is just above your knees. If you sit down, the base moves down accordingly. That means, then, if you are sitting in a chair, the base is on the floor, or at least very close to that. If you are sitting on the ground, approximately one half of the male tetrahedron is in the ground.

The base of the female tetrahedron is always at the solar plexus, whether you are standing or sitting. If you are standing, the apex of the female tetrahedron is one hand length into the ground. If you are sitting on a chair, the apex moves down accordingly. If you are sitting on the ground, more than one half of the female tetrahedron is in the ground.

As you continue to do this meditation, your ability to "see" the tetrahedrons, white light, tube, and spheres will improve.

When I began, I had a very limited ability to visualize the tetrahedrons. I could only sense the tube and the growing ball of prana as being in front of me. I was a little better at seeing the light. This has all improved to the point where these fields are now part of me, an extension of my body and being, if you will.

Practicing sacred geometry has helped immensely. As I got into it, I learned this by actually doing the drawings. I don't think there is any other way to really get it.

The geometry not only helped my meditation but also greatly facilitated an integration of my left and right brain into the oneness of the eternal spirit.

One way of explaining this is that I have a greatly increased ability to hold every experience in my life as an opportunity rather than as something either to be avoided or made wrong. This leads to the increased awareness that everything is unfolding just as it should, that I am getting exactly what I need in every moment.

It is one thing to know this conceptually; it is something

else again to know it as your living experience. For me it clearly was the missing piece.

How long it takes to master this breathing exercise—that is, to remember on every breath your intimate connection to the source—is of course different for each individual. Drunvalo says he had to be reminded by the angels on a regular basis, and that it took him twelve years to master it.

I found that it took me sixteen to seventeen months to master the first fourteen breaths, and the process continues.

I have made tremendous progress. I am increasingly aware of the energy field around my body and the enormous amount of safety and protection it provides.

I have also combined this breathing with my rebirthing. Now when I rebirth myself I always take the prana in through the top of my head so it passes through my pineal gland, while I also bring it up through the perineum.

This has been a gradual process. When I first began I had little more than faith and a solid commitment. Now it is obvious to me that I have an enormously increased ability to rebirth myself and others.

I feel my pineal gland waking up, and I feel and "see" the light in me more and more. Unity of being is becoming more and more a living presence. I am becoming increasingly a conscious breather, that is, remembering with each breath my intimate connection with all life.

Activating the Merkaba

Breaths fifteen through seventeen are the ones that set the counter-rotating fields of the merkaba in motion.

Until recently, the instructions from Drunvalo were not to attempt these last three breaths until you have made contact with your higher self and have been given permission from within to proceed. The new directive, as a result of the incredible rate of our evolution, is to proceed whenever you feel ready.

As you prepare for the fifteenth breath, keeping the same mudra, be aware of the whole star tetrahedron, and remember, there are three identical star tetrahedral fields superimposed over each other (see p. 27).

The first star tetrahedron is neutral in nature and is literally the physical body. It is locked in place at the base of the spine and does not rotate. Like the other two star tetrahedral fields, it is placed around the body according to maleness or femaleness.

The second star tetrahedron is electrical in nature, male, and rotates to the left. It is literally the mental body.

The third star tetrahedron is magnetic in nature, female, and rotates to the right. It is the emotional body.

On the seven-second inhale of the fifteenth breath, say to yourself, "equal speed." This will start the two whole-star tetrahedral fields spinning in opposite directions at the same speed. This means that for every complete rotation to the left of the mental (male) star tetrahedron, there will be a complete rotation to the right of the emotional (female) star tetrahedron.

You exhale on breaths fifteen through seventeen in the same "forced air" manner as you did for breath number ten.

As you exhale, the two sets of star tetrahedrons start spinning, instantly reaching one-third the speed of light.

On the inhale for the sixteenth breath, say to yourself, "thirty-four, twenty-one."

This will start the two star tetrahedrons spinning in opposite directions at a ratio of thirty-four spins to the left for the mental (male) star tetrahedron, and twenty-one spins to the right for the emotional (female) star tetrahedron.

On the forced-air exhale, the two sets of star tetrahedrons instantly increase in speed from one-third to two-thirds the speed of light. Also, a fifty-five-foot-diameter disk forms around the body centered at the base of the spine. This disk, along with the sphere of energy that is centered on the two sets of star tetrahedrons, creates a shape around the body that looks much like a flying saucer. This is the merkaba. However, at this point the field is not stable. More speed is needed, and the next breath provides that.

As you inhale on breath seventeen, say to yourself, "nine-tenths the speed of light." This will stabilize your merkaba field by increasing the speed to nine-tenths the speed of light. This breath will also tune you perfectly to our third-dimensional universe, where electrons rotate around atoms at exactly nine-tenths the speed of light.

As mentioned above, you exhale in the same forced-air manner as you did for breaths fifteen and sixteen.

There is ultimately one more breath in this meditation, the eighteenth breath. This is the breath that, when taken, will carry you through the speed of light and into the fourth dimension. This breath can only be given to you from within, from direct contact from your higher self.

In order to ensure that you properly learn the merkaba meditation, I highly recommend the "Flower of Life" workshop.

Let us keep in mind what is *really* happening. In the context of the bigger picture, we are in the process of moving from one world to the next, from the third dimension to the tenth, eleventh, or twelfth overtone of the fourth dimension or, as the Native Americans would say, from the fourth to the fifth world. That means we are all in transition; we are all going through tremendous change. For many of us, our old world is falling apart while the new one is not yet firmly in place. It also means that we are in the process of completing the past. We must clean up the mess we have made before we can move from one world to the next. My purpose is to see to it that our journey from one dimension to the next is a safe, smooth ride, and to empower you in a like manner.

It is in that spirit that I offer my two workshops, the "Flower of Life" and "Nothing to Something." In the "Flower of Life," you are given information that has been kept secret for more than three thousand years. This includes everything you always wanted to know about Atlantis, Lemuria, Egypt, dolphins, conspiracies, and our intergalactic connections. We also work with the universal language of sacred geometry, which is used to show the mind the Unity of Being. Ultimately, the workshop is about the teaching of the merkaba, the activation of the energy fields around the body, which serves as a field of protection and also as a vehicle of ascension. In other words, you learn how to move from the third to the fourth dimension, bringing your body with you.

The information given in the "Flower of Life" is designed to facilitate the awakening of unity consciousness in the individual, that is, the movement from polarity into unity. When a group of like-minded people comes together in this setting, an experience of unity consciousness is created unlike anything I have ever seen.

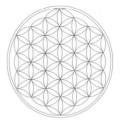

The Philadelphia Experiment

At least on the surface, the Philadelphia Experiment (officially known as Project Rainbow) was a top-secret military experiment that attempted to make a battleship invisible. Yes, invisible! Did you see the movie of the same name? The experiment happened in 1943, right in the middle of World War II. Making a battleship invisible is really not that hard to do. All you have to do is take it into the next dimensional overtone and it is invisible to everyone on this dimensional level. Drunvalo says this is something that everyone can do; it's the cloaking device of the Klingons. The technology for the Philadelphia Experiment came to us from the Greys. We wanted a cloaking device to win the war, but they had very different reasons for giving us this technology, which I will discuss later.

To make something invisible, or to go to the next higher dimensional overtone, you have to create counter-rotating fields of energy at very specific speeds. In the experiment, the government scientists got counter-rotating fields going based on a star tetrahedron. When you go from one dimensional world to another, the counter-rotating fields shoot from nine-tenths the speed of light to the actual speed of light, which involves an incredibly complex series of whole-number harmonics that build upon each other.

The visual experience of this is that the space around you turns to a red fog and takes the shape of a flying saucer. The colors then progress through the whole rainbow very quickly, going from red to orange, yellow, and green, blue to purple to ultraviolet purple, and then to a blinding white light that slowly recedes. Any physical objects will appear to be made out of gold, then the gold will slowly become translucent and then transparent. At that point you can see right through things. Then you are into blackness and at this point you make a 90-degree shift, which is done in two distinct 45-degree shifts. Different dimensional worlds are all separated by 90-degree angles. After the 90-degree shift you reappear in a whole new world on a different dimensional level.

The Philadelphia Experiment, regardless of whatever was actually done, was a true-life episode carried out by the U.S. Navy in 1943. It involved the battleship *USS Eldridge*. The scientists working on the project were just trying to make the ship invisible to radar, not totally invisible. In this experiment the colors went from red to orange to yellow to green; that much didn't take very long but they never got beyond that stage. It was like taking a jet a few hundred feet off the ground and then shutting down the motors; in other words, the experiment interdimensionally crashed. The battleship with everyone on it disappeared out of the Philadelphia Navy Yard for about four hours. When they reappeared some of the crew members were found literally imbedded in the deck, two were found in bulkheads, some were on fire, some didn't come back at all, and some were repeatedly materializing and dematerializing. The survivors were all completely disoriented.

Two particular individuals on the battleship jumped off in the middle of the experiment thinking they could swim away, but when they landed they found themselves not in the Philadelphia harbor but on Long Island, New York, in

1983. The reason they landed at this time was a similar experiment, called the Montauk Project,[1] that was done in 1983 and was connected to the 1943 Philadelphia Experiment. These two individuals were brothers named Duncan and Edward Cameron.

Both experiments were conducted on August 12th of their respective years. According to Al Bielek, who claims to be Edward Cameron, one of the two men who jumped off the *USS Eldridge,*[2] there are four bio-fields of the planet and all four peak out every twenty years on the 12th of August—1943, 1963, 1983, 2003, etc. This creates a peak of magnetic energies at these times and also coupled the two experiments. The energies were sufficient to create a hyper-space field, and caused the battleship *USS Eldridge* to slip into hyper-space during the 1943 experiment.

Al Bielek says the linking of the two experiments, which ripped a huge hole in space-time, was caused deliberately by the Greys who worked on the 1983 experiment. They did this to put a rift in the fabric of space-time so that large numbers of aliens and ships could come through. Evidently the rift was necessary to get large ships through and make a mass (silent) invasion of the United States. From that invasion came the joint U.S.-Grey treaty. In linear time, the 1983 Montauk Project came after the 1943 Philadelphia Experiment, but this experiment created a time-loop in which the way we conceive of linear time chronology no longer applies.

Drunvalo has said that he met Duncan Cameron through New York Jets coach Pete Carroll. He also met a former government employee named Preston Nichols who was an engineer on the Montauk Project. Duncan was able to see the rotating fields around Drunvalo, something few people can do, and Drunvalo could see rotating fields around Duncan, although they were way out of balance.

It was Duncan's spine that was used to run the fields in

both the Philadelphia and Montauk experiments. That is just what life forms do—whales and dolphins, for example. The head of the pod uses his spinal column to set up an electromagnetic field around him, and everyone else in the pod is connected to that field. It is as though there is just one body with many separate cells in it. Whatever the lead being does, everyone else follows. This explains the phenomenon of beached whales: if the lead whale ends up on the beach for whatever reason, all the other whales in the pod will follow. They are acting as one body.

Anyway, Duncan Cameron was used in both experiments. The hole in space-time has created huge vortices of energy in the fourth dimension which, according to Drunvalo, our government is very worried about. If these vortices of energy appear in our dimension, huge areas of the Earth could be destroyed—even the entire planet. However, according to Drunvalo, higher beings are not concerned about this; according to them there is no problem.

The Monuments of Mars

It was the Greys who set up these time experiments, not our government. It wasn't even really our government who followed their lead; it was something called the "secret government" and it was not done for the purpose of making a ship invisible, although that was the ostensible reason. The Greys had a much larger agenda having to do with Mars. Remember, one million years ago their ancestors were successful with a similar experiment almost identical to this one; in fact, they left the monuments on Mars mathematically describing that experiment. These monuments were first photographed by NASA's *Viking* in 1976.

The *Viking* photographs show what looks like a face on Mars in an area known as Cydonia. *Viking* also photographed a five-sided pyramid, several four-sided pyramids, and other distinctive objects.

A number of people, including Vincent di Pietro and Gregory Molenaar, NASA subcontractees, and later Richard Hoagland,[3] got the *Viking* photographs from NASA and released them. After interpreting the photographs of monuments on Mars, which NASA was very reluctant to acknowledge, Hoagland, along with geologist Erol Torun, began exploring the geometry of the objects in them. As he learned more about the science of sacred geometry and studied in great depth the images, he discovered that the angles between the pyramids described mathematically in great detail a tetrahedron inscribed in a sphere. When you have a tetrahedron inscribed in a sphere with the apex placed at either pole, the base will touch the sphere at 19.47 degrees (rounded off to 19.5 degrees) of the latitude opposite that pole. If you have a star tetrahedron (two back-to-back tetrahedrons) inscribed in a sphere, the two bases will touch the sphere at 19.5 degrees north and south (Fig. 13–1). Richard Hoagland found this angle repeated over and over in the images of the pyramids

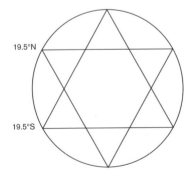

Figure 13–1. A star tetrahedron inscribed in a sphere. The two bases touch the sphere at 19.5° north and south latitude.

on Mars. This turns out, of course, to be a very significant angle.

Hoagland also studied images of Jupiter, Saturn, and Neptune taken by various unmanned NASA spacecraft. He found that the red spot on Jupiter sits at 19.5 degrees latitude. The great dark spot on Neptune is at 19.5 degrees latitude and researchers believe there is a similar dark spot on Uranus at 19.5 degrees south latitude. On Saturn there are two cloud bands at 19.5 degrees latitude north and south. In addition, when you track sunspot activity, its primary focus seems to be 19.5 degrees north and south latitudes. Thus, there are major concentrations of planetary energy at 19.5 degrees north and south. On Earth, the Maunakea Volcano on the Hawaiian Islands falls at 19.5 degrees north.[4]

According to Drunvalo, there are actually three star tetrahedral fields around all planets and they are rotating and creating electromagnetic fields. NASA and Hoagland are at present time only becoming aware of one of these fields.

NASA did not want us to know about the discovery of pyramids on Mars and has done everything it can to ridicule interested parties, even those within their organization. Why does NASA not want us to know about this? It has to do with the secret government, the Greys, and Earth changes which will be presented later.

Free Energy Machines

There now exist working free energy machines, and these are based upon this technology of rotating energy fields. One is called the N machine, which is, according to Drunvalo, functioning in India and will probably be released soon. These machines can provide virtually an infinite supply of electricity for just a few hundred dollars. They never wear out.

Nikola Tesla tried to give the world free energy a long time ago. According to George C. Andrews in *Extra-Terrestrial Friends and Foes,*

> Tesla intended to offer to the world free and inex-haustible energy, via the tapping of the electricity from the earth and atmosphere, then broadcasting it through a wave carrier, just like radio. That break-through was obviously not to the taste of the tycoons, owners of elec-tric plants, generator and electric cable manufacturers, not to mention the oil kings. Came 1910, and poor Tesla was laughed at and ridiculed, and the people who had supported him financially were forced by mightier play-ers to demand immediate repayment of the invested money. Regarded as a lunatic by the public, deserted by all, and utterly broke, Nikola Tesla died in the United States in 1943.[5]

So the powers-that-be haven't wanted us to know about these free energy machines either, but it is inevitable. Accord-ing to Drunvalo they have been presented to the United Nations and it is now only a matter of time before this infor-mation becomes public.

Venus

Drunvalo says there is another monument complex on Venus that NASA also knows about. In January 1985, NASA dis-covered the Venus complex, which is identical to the one at Giza in Egypt: three pyramids, a Sphinx—exactly the same. There are over 200 photographs of this Cytherean complex. Drunvalo claims to have talked directly to some of the peo-ple involved in this.

The Mental Health Committee of the U.S., a twelve-per-son committee consulted by NASA whenever it comes up with evidence indicating there is life on other planets, gave permission in May 1985 to release this information about Venus to the public. This meant that NASA was bound by law to report it.

NASA broadcast the information on a single television station in Florida one time and that was it. Of course nobody would believe that. By putting this information out only once NASA fulfilled its legal requirement to make the information public and was able to get away with supressing it after this initial revelation.

Immediately after this incident, NASA sent a vessel back to Venus and mapped over 90 percent of the surface, in an attempt to see what else was there. That was only the third-dimensional aspect, however; they obviously don't know how to map the fourth-dimensional aspects of planets. When you go to any planet you have to tune to the right dimensional level to find anything significant. Only certain dimensional levels are alive. There is no life on Venus on the third dimension.

However, on the fourth dimension, Venus is a well-populated, beautiful planet. It is peopled by the Hathor race, the most intelligent and advanced race by far in our solar system. They are far more advanced than humans, the Greys, or the Nefilim.

The Hathor are Christ-consciousness beings. They stand ten to sixteen feet tall and base all their science on sound currents coming from the throat. They are beings of pure light and tremendous love. They have been working with the Egyptians and with us for a long time. The pyramid complex on Venus had to do with the constant back-and-forth communication and travel the Hathors and Egyptians once had with each other.

There are also complexes on the moon, ancient Egyptian as well as present-day secret government complexes. We have three small bases on the dark side of the moon. The secret

Project Clementine, conducted by the SDI-affiliated branch of NASA, involved the launch of a spacecraft to this region on the day of President Clinton's State of the Union address in 1994.

Let me return to the Philadelphia Experiment and the real reason the Greys wanted to carry it out. When the Martian atmosphere was on the brink of destruction, the Martians (the ancestors of the present-day Greys), built a complex at Cydonia for the purpose of creating an external merkaba, a time-space vehicle which would enable them to project themselves into the future. They not only laid out this complex at Cydonia to show mathematically how they did it, but the complex was also the actual mechanism that they used to do it. This occurred at least a million Earth years ago, according to Thoth. The Martians were successful and projected themselves to Atlantis approximately 65,000 Earth years ago.

The descendants of the Martians attempted this experiment again 16,000 years ago, but this time they lost control of it, ripping open dimensional levels and pulling spirits from lower dimensional levels into Atlantis, where they inhabited the bodies of the Atlanteans.

This failed experiment was attempted in a building that is now on the ocean floor in an area known as the Bermuda Triangle. In this building are counter-rotating star tetrahedral fields creating a huge synthetic merkaba field.

One of the triangular tips of these fields is sticking out of the ocean, and is completely out of control.

In order for the merkaba field to be under control, the counter-clockwise field has to be rotating faster. But the clockwise field occasionally rotates faster, and this is what causes all the distortions. Planes and ships that have disappeared in this area have literally gone into different dimensional levels.

There are also distortions extending into vast regions of space. This is a big problem that extends way beyond Earth.

This problem is also affecting the Greys, so they along with other races are here with permission trying to fix this.

Drunvalo doesn't know how many other comparable experiments the Greys have tried, but they definitely undertook one in 1913. They tried again in 1943 with the Philadelphia Experiment and in 1983 with the Montauk Project. There will be at least one more of these experiments in our future.

Al Bielek, who claims to have been involved with the Montauk Project, said the scientists working on the project developed the ability to travel easily in time. They could go as far into the past or future as they wanted. Drunvalo presents the actuality a bit differently. According to him they could go back in time as far as a million years and then they ran into a wall. They could also go forward in time until the year 2012, where they ran into another wall. The reason for this is that the first experiment was one million years ago, so the Greys can't go beyond it, and they also can't go beyond their last experiment, which will be around 2012. This is because all of these experiments are interconnected, not just Philadelphia and Montauk, but all of them!

The Greys are trying to solve certain problems and have been given free rein to do so from higher aspects of life. Life is about creating a win-win situation for everyone, not about wiping out the Greys or anyone else; it is about creating something that works for everyone.

Cattle Mutilations

Another aspect of the Greys' experimentation on this planet involves cattle mutilations. The reason the Greys were cutting up cattle—and I realize this is past-tense—was to try to understand sexual energy. The Greys stopped being sexual themselves long ago and only continued reproducing via test tubes.

Over the past twenty years, there have been thousands of reported cases of mutilations of cattle (and other animals as well) all over the world. Linda Moulton Howe, one of the prime investigators of these incidents, did an ABC television special on the mutilations called "The Strange Harvest" and also wrote the book called *An Alien Harvest.*[6] She first thought that the U.S. government was responsible, but after more research, she concluded it had to be someone more technologically advanced than our government. She found that the incisions were made with incredibly accurate lasers, beyond our present capability. Furthermore, the cows were placed back on the ground with every single red blood cell removed, something humans can't accomplish.

The Greys were also abducting humans and conducting experiments on them—in numbers far beyond the limited basis permitted by their agreement with the government. This again was done primarily to understand our sexual and emotional energy. According to Drunvalo, the Greys have now left the Earth, so hopefully these abductions have ceased.

The Greys now realize that to get out of the trap they created for themselves by separating themselves from the source of life, they have to get back their emotional bodies. Unfortunately, the only way they know how to do this is by studying us intellectually, which of course will never work.

Originally the Greys were created much like us, with their emotional bodies intact. It was their allegiance to the Lucifer rebellion that alienated them from the reality of unity. They took external machinery too far, and this just doesn't work. It has been tried many times in the universe, always with disastrous results. The construction of ships to cross the stars and robots to do all the work always robs species of their emotional bodies, which is their main source of power.

You can create the merkaba externally. It requires only knowledge, no love, emotion, or feelings. What you get is a

UFO. All UFOs, or flying saucers, are based on the principles of the external merkaba. The problem is this separates
you from the source of life and you eventually lose your emotional body altogether. When you manufacture the merkaba
externally you do not have to use any emotion, you don't
have to use any love; nothing from the emotional body is
needed. The mental mind is all that is needed. What this creates is a being who ultimately only knows logic and doesn't
have an emotional body.

There is also another problem or fatal flaw with the external merkaba; there is a limitation on how high you can ascend
dimensionally. The great wall of voidness between the octaves
was intentionally created to require emotion in order to pass
through. No UFOs or any form of external machinery can
make it through. This is a detail Lucifer missed—Lucifer, the
fourth angel to separate from God, who attempted to base
creation on an external template. One million years ago Mars
was in the last death throes from the effects of an earlier
Lucifer-type rebellion. Many planets and whole areas of space
were destroyed as a result. The Martians also succeeded to
the point where they had no emotional body or capacity to
love. They were based totally on logic and ended up destroy-
ing their planet. When they projected themselves in time to
Atlantis, they brought their sickness with them to Earth.

The present Lucifer rebellion began in this galaxy about
200,000 years ago. The Greys are a quintessential aspect of
this rebellion. They now exist on hundreds of planets in the
galaxy but are mostly concentrated around Alnilam, the middle star in the belt of Orion. They are also related to the Martians, who are among their ancestors. The Greys are a race
without an emotional body and they are dying because of
the fatal flaw associated with basing creation on the external merkaba. They are trapped in their present level of exis-

tence. They cannot ascend any higher or go to the next octave of existence because they have separated themselves from the reality to such a degree that they don't even know what love is. This means they can't "feel" their way through creation. They are now aware of this problem; they understand it logically but don't know how to change it.

In their sexual experiments with humans, the Greys attempted to blend themselves or put their essence into our species so that maybe something of themselves would survive. They cloned another race on this planet through which they hope their genes will continue. As cloning experts, the Greys have done extensive experimenting on humans for a long time. They have made many experimental models of humans in search of the perfect one. They are doing this because they are a dying breed and they know it. Their experiments with humans are an attempt to preserve something of themselves by creating a Grey-Human hybrid. They realize that they are not going to make it, that their particular life form is terminating. The universe has allowed the Greys to do this because all of us on planet Earth are deeply implicated with them from the Martian connection in Atlantis.

There are at least five other extraterrestrial races involved in this drama. For instance, other dimensional beings are making sure the Greys don't overstep themselves as they were wont in the past. In fact, according to Drunvalo, not too long ago they blatantly tried to wipe us out by opening up the fourth dimensional level too quickly. If their attempt had been successful, it would have blown us away.

Accessing higher dimensional levels always needs to happen slowly and organically. When the Greys attempted to force this process they established a grid around the Earth and were about to open up a dimensional window. The window had the power to work both ways, so in order to make sure the ascended masters of the Earth didn't stop them they made the window infinitesimally small and opened up the grid randomly at tiny dots all over the planet. However, by using love the ascended masters intuitively interpreted the random pattern, and when the window opened they projected love back through it and blocked the dimensional hole with light. The Greys were absolutely silent for about three months after this.

This happened about three or four years ago, and the Greys knew that it was about their last chance here. They saw that our human consciousness was nearing readiness to gain control over what could be called the dreamtime of the planet. This is in fact what happened when the woman from Peru went into Christ-consciousness, raised the ship that was buried in the Earth, and cast her spell on the Greys. The Greys knew when that happened we would gain control, not them.

A final point regarding the Lucifer rebellion that I intimated earlier but would like to emphasize now is that viewing any of this as good or bad is only our limited interpretation. We are stuck here on the third dimension in polarity consciousness. From a higher level of existence all of this is just an organic process that has both good and bad aspects to it. It has purpose and is leading us somewhere.

Notes

1. Preston B. Nichols and Peter Moon, *The Montauk Project, Experiments In Time* (Westbury, New York: Sky Books, 1992).

2. Al Bielek and Vladimir Terziski, "The Philadelphia teleportation and time-travel experiments of the Illuminati." 120-minute videotape (The American Academy of Dissident Sciences, May 1992).

3. Richard C. Hoagland, *The Monuments of Mars: A City on the Edge of Forever* (Berkeley, CA: North Atlantic Books, 1987).

4. Richard C. Hoagland, "Hoagland's Mars: The NASA-Cydonia Briefings," Volume One, 83-minute videotape (Hoagland and Curley, 1991).

5. George C. Andrews, *Extra-Terrestrial Friends and Foes* (Libum, GA: IllumiNet Press, 1993), p. 211.

6. Linda Moulton Howe, *An Alien Harvest: Further Evidence Linking Animal Mutilations And Human Abductions To Alien Life Forms* (Littleton, CO: Linda Moulton Howe Productions, 1989).

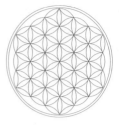

14

1972

To begin this story we must go far back in time to when Thoth and other ascended masters were synthetically creating the Christ-consciousness grid on this planet to heal what had happened between the Martians and the Earthlings in Atlantis. When the ascended masters began their construction of the grid, they made the hole in Egypt that connects to the flower of life in the Halls of Amenti and activated their geomancy with sacred points all over the world. The ascended masters then calculated that we would matriculate into the fourth dimension by the winter of 1998, and at that time only a very few people would make it. There was nothing unusual about this experiment of creating the Christ-consciousness grid synthetically. Apparently it is done on a regular basis— that is, jumping planets up or down dimensional levels. No one in the universe paid any particular attention to this experiment; it was no big deal.

However, about 200 years ago the Sirians, who are our father aspect, became aware of a high possibility that we were not going to make it at all. They foresaw an event that was going to happen in 1972, and they knew that we had to be at the fourth dimensional level of awareness by then in order to survive. If we were at that level by 1972 there would be no problem, but if not, everything would be wiped out— the entire planet. And, as time passed, it more and more seemed as if we would not reach that consciousness level.

The Sirians did not want to see us wiped out. We are, in a certain sense, their children and they have that special parental love connection with us. They started searching for a way to solve this problem but were unsuccessful. There was no known way to get a planet at our level of awareness through the changes that were coming. When this had happened in the past it meant that the planet was destroyed. The Sirians kept on looking, however, and eventually they discovered that someone in a faraway galaxy had conceived of an idea that might work, but had never been tried. It was still not totally certain that we were not going to make it—consciousness can and does make quantum leaps all the time— but the Sirians were assuming the worst. So they went ahead and prepared everything necessary to implement the idea or experiment that they had come upon.

They created a living vehicle that was fifty miles long, cigar-shaped, black, and seamless with both carbon and silicon life forms on it merged into one. The whole thing was a self-aware living unit. It had a transparent area on one end and was manned by about 300 to 350 men and women of the Sirian race from the third planet. They wore white uniforms with gold emblems. Dedicating as much time to this project as was necessary, they also made eight little flying saucer- type vehicles or ships that were to be unmanned; these were approximately twelve to twenty feet in length. The Sirians assembled this all together, worked out all its possibilities, then set it aside and waited.

Meanwhile, back on Earth in early 1972, Drunvalo was directed to Canada as soon as he got here. He had to make a secret connection with a man named David Suzuki. Suzuki is a very highly disciplined person who works on many different levels. He studied genetics not by looking through a microscope but by looking through a telescope. He believed in the principle "as above, so below." If you are looking at really big things you can see all motions more clearly. He watched the movements of asteroids and applied that to his understanding of genetics.

Suzuki was also interested in the activity of our sun and had a team of people watching it all the time. He knew that one day in 1950, researchers had witnessed a phenomenon that was unknown in human experience. A spiraling light came off the sun and went rapidly right past the Earth. They had no idea what this was, but it was an indication of something unusual occurring.

As the Earth rotates on its axis, the axis itself wobbles, creating several cycles—the slow 25,920–year precession, and another wobble that is the inclination itself oscillating back and forth, which takes about 46,000 years. There are also other wobbles; one in particular takes fourteen years. According to Suzuki, we were on the furthermost point of this wobble in 1950. When the spiral went flying past the Earth the area subtended by the wobble began to widen, the equivalent of a top slowing down. It took researchers fourteen years of study before concluding that this change in the wobble would lead to a shifting of the poles, giving Earth a new north and south pole. By 1964 they were pretty certain of this.

Suzuki's team studied the data for four more years before they acted. In 1968 they were convinced the pole shift was imminent. Suzuki published a paper that was first distributed only to the Canadian government, then to the United States and most other governments, saying that we were going to have a new north and south pole. He said the spiral of light was coming off the sun like clockwork every three years, only it was increasing in intensity each time. From all their calculations of the past eighteen years they had concluded that sometime in 1972 between August and November the energy level would be such that there would be an explosion on the sun, an explosion unparalleled in our experience. They predicted there would be another explosion in 1984, and very soon after that we would lose our present north and south poles.

The actual event happened on August 7, 1972. From our observation—and we didn't know of course that the Sirians had intervened—it was the biggest thing that we had ever seen. Anthony R. Curtis, in his book *The Space Almanac,* called it "the most intense solar storm ever recorded."[1] According to "Science News": "The early days of August saw a severe disturbance on the sun that produced four major flares between August 2 and August 7.... The ones recorded in early August were among the most major ever recorded.... The August 7 flare ran the X-ray sensors off the scale...."[2] The solar wind, which has an average velocity of 500 km/sec., or a million miles per hour, got up to 2½ million miles an hour for three days, then it dropped down to 1½ million miles an hour for thirty days. This was considered impossible, yet it happened. Accounts of the event were published in all the major scientific literature of the world and many of the major newspapers, but scientists didn't know what it meant; all they did was publish the data. After six months, David Suzuki called a worldwide scientific meeting to discuss the implications of this explosion. Drunvalo left him about three months before the meeting so he doesn't know what happened at the meeting. What he does know is that previous to the meeting—that is, from August to November 1972—there was a great amount of information published and written about this. After the meeting in June or July of 1973, there was a total worldwide blackout, just as if the great event had never happened.

If the Sirians had not intervened, the explosion would have definitely killed us all. It would have killed everything on the planet right down to the level of microbes and algae. What really happened was that our sun was about to expand in a giant red pulse out to the orbit of Jupiter or thereabouts. For five billion years or so, ours has been a hydrogen sun, where two hydrogen atoms fuse together to make helium. This has been the source of all the light and life on Earth. When the helium that has been building up reaches critical mass, you get another reaction, with three helium atoms coming together to form carbon. At that moment, the sun pulses. A shifting of the sun's poles also took place as a result of a bubble, two-thirds the size of the sun, forming on its surface. If we had been prepared for this, that is, consciously prepared—if we were at the Christ-consciousness level or higher—we could have just tuned to it and it would have been a beautiful trip. But since we had fallen so far in consciousness from the events in Atlantis 16,000 years ago and had not yet moved into Christ-consciousness, we certainly were not prepared.

At the time, 144,000 different races from the other dimensional levels came in here to assist. By mid-January 1972, about 80,000 of them had already arrived. They had a very intense discussion among themselves on the subject of the impending red pulse and about 79,900 of these cultures said, "There is no hope, there is no way, there is not a prayer of the humans surviving. Let's get out of here." They went home because noninterference was their policy. The other hundred or so cultures—the Pleiadians, the Aldebarans, the Arcturans and others led by the Sirians—decided to stay and help.

The Sirians not only had the hardware and software in place but also ambassadors. The moment the situation was declared hopeless they sent ambassadors to Galactic Command to ask for permission to carry out their experiment. If anyone at all, even just one person, were to survive this explosion of the sun, the Sirians would have been refused. But because no one on Earth was going to survive, they did receive permission. They were first asked by Galactic Command how many survivors they thought there would be as a result of their experiment. They didn't really know but said, "Probably at least two but no more than ten will make it." A key condition for receiving permission was the belief that at least one person would survive. In truth, as this was a radical thing that had never been tried before, they didn't really know how many would survive.

After receiving permission the Sirians immediately went to work and within thirty days had everything in place. They launched the large cigar-shaped object just outside the membrane of consciousness of the Earth, at 440,000 miles out, and they placed it one overtone higher so it was invisible to us. They placed the eight small flying saucer-type ships on the apexes of the eight tetrahedral points—that is, the eight points of the star tetrahedron around the Earth. There is a star tetrahedron inscribed in the Earth. There is also a much bigger one, around 10,000 miles above the surface. The points are the chakra system of the planet. Again, these were set one dimensional overtone higher than the Earth. Then from the cigar-shaped ship they shot a beam of laser light, the likes of which we do not have. The beam was about eight inches in diameter, made up of little segments of different colored digital light moving, of course, at the speed of light. This light was coming from one dimensional world into another.

The beam entered into the North Pole and hit the little flying saucer-type ship that was at that tetrahedral point. From there, the immense amount of information contained in the laser light was translated into three primary rays—red, blue, and green—that were beamed to the next three ships. These ships repeated this and sent the rays to the next three ships until the rays ended up at the South Pole. At the South Pole they were translated back into information and shot into the center of the Earth. From the center of the Earth, by refraction, the information came out in little tiny beams of light by the billions, all over the whole planet. As these beams of light came out through the center of the Earth they connected to all the humans and animals on the planet.

Remember, the Sirians had to protect us from a wall of flame and this is how they did it. Not only did they have to protect us, but they also had to do it in such a way that we didn't know we were being protected. Our knowing would have completely changed the human equation. They also had to speed up our evolution so we could get to where we could handle a wall of flame. They set a holographic field around the Earth; then they set up a holographic field around each person and animal. They then began to program events into these holographic fields. In the first few months they didn't change anything, they just got control. Then they pro-grammed our sky into a hologram and kept everything going as though nothing unusual were happening. Then they began to program events into our lives so that we would evolve as rapidly as possible. At the same time, they were protecting us from the wall of flame.

From the summer of 1972 to the summer of 1974 we were moving in an entirely new direction. We began to accelerate in our evolution. Then it started to get out of hand; we began to *really* accelerate. This experiment was much more successful than they ever imagined. Instead of ten or so making it through, the number is now up to 1½ billion or so people who will make it through to the next level. We have obviously all been protected from the wall of flame; we're still here. The Sirian intervention also bought time for the synthetic Christ-consciousness grid to be completed. Without the Christ-consciousness grid, no one can make it to the next level of consciousness. This grid was completed on February 4, 1989.

Normally, when a planet goes into Christ-consciousness only a very few people initially make it through to live and understand the new reality. The rest drop down to a lower level of consciousness and only over a very long period of time the initial few pull the rest up until the whole planet reaches Christ-consciousness.

There are, as well, different levels of Christ-consciousness. The levels of Christ-consciousness in the fourth dimension are the tenth, eleventh, and twelfth overtones. It usually takes a long period of time for a planet to evolve through those stages. The first two overtones of the fourth dimension contain the astral plane, where very powerful thought forms have taken on a life of their own. The third overtone is where most people go when they die, the fourth contains faeries and tree spirits. The angelic realms are from the seventh to the ninth overtones. It isn't until you reach the tenth overtone of the fourth dimension that you attain Christ-consciousness. It is to one of these higher overtones of the fourth dimension that we as a planet are headed.

The geometry of the consciousness grid around any planet changes as the consciousness of the planet changes. These changes are normally very rare. Usually small changes occur over thousands of years. Changes on the grid around the Earth are now happening hourly. This has attracted the attention of beings from all parts of the galaxy. Because we are inside the system, it is difficult for us to know how fast we are moving. But for anyone outside observing us, it is obvious. What is happening here is unheard of; it has gotten to the point where we are on interdimensional galactic television. That's why the two higher overtones are like a parking lot. Everyone is tuned into us to monitor this event because they know that whatever happens to us here will affect them, too. All life everywhere will be touched by this. According to Thoth, an analogy for the speed at which we are evolving is one of a newborn baby becoming an adult in fifteen minutes. This is totally unique; there are no memory patterns for it anywhere, even on the Melchizedek level. It appears to be the most successful experiment that anyone anywhere has ever conducted. Drunvalo now suspects that this may have been in the mind of God from the very beginning.

However, the ascended masters don't know what the outcome will be. Thoth wanted Drunvalo to be very clear about this. It thus far appears to be a very successful experiment, but the ascended masters keep figuring out game plans that become obsolete before they can even implement them. Originally Thoth and other ascended masters thought the planet would reach critical mass around the last week of August 1990 or the first week of September 1990, and that by the spring of 1991 we would go into another dimensional level. The ascended masters said they would then bond together, leave the Earth in a ball of light, and go into another level of consciousness. That would pull us up and serve as the trigger for everyone to ascend.

Instead, what happened in August 1990 was that Iraq invaded Kuwait. The major nations of the Earth did band together, but in preparation for war against Iraq. Because of this the ascended masters held off. We created planetary unity of a sort by banding together against one man in one country. This was unique in our history. Never before in human history has essentially the entire planet melded together against one person. Even the world wars were very different from this. Because of the Iraqi war, the ascended masters created a new game plan whereby thirty-two of them would go off at one time in a group merkaba. They actually went through the great wall of voidness and into the next octave. This is how Thoth left on May 4, 1991. That would bring us up a little bit at a time instead of all at once. Every time they do this there will be a rapid expansion in our consciousness. They are timing these events now.

Before Thoth left here he told Drunvalo that he suspects we will not go through the sudden and violent shifting of the poles that usually accompanies a planet's change of consciousness. Rather, we will go through a series of steps with our eyes open and we will do it very harmonically. The ascended masters are going to try to make this a controlled shift of consciousness.

Let's return to late August and early September 1990 for a moment. We *did* reach critical mass. We had the necessary seven to ten percent or roughly 500 million people who had opened up enough that they would go through. Ascension should have taken place.

The numbers kept growing. We went way beyond critical mass. Then in January 1992 another phenomenon took place — for the first time in 16,000 years, the light on the planet was more powerful than the darkness, and it still wasn't igniting. Something else was clearly happening—a cold-fusion process, if you will.

However, because the light was now in control, the Sirians decided we should be given back our power.

The programming of the Earth (how the events take place in our world) was given back to us. Since January 1992 what occurs on the planet is up to us completely. If we could just understand the nature of the situation, that our thoughts and feelings are creating the reality, we could change very rapidly.

Drunvalo believes that all previous predictions regarding the future of the Earth are no longer valid. The Sirian experiment of 1972 changed everything. Nostradamus was very accurate in his predictions up until 1972, and since then he has fallen way off. Suzuki predicted a pole shift in 1984; he was sure of it. When 1984 came, we were in a totally different place. Thoth believes that we are going to have the most unique experience that life has ever had. Most likely, by 2012 or before, every last person left on the planet will ascend into the next dimensional level together.

There will be people dying all along, and those who do will go into Christ-consciousness through resurrection. We will be making this shift as a conscious planet, as though we were a million years further advanced. Many higher aspects of life everywhere are begging to come down here either through birth or as walk-ins to directly experience this because it is so unusual. It appears that we have made it in a really big way, and we will soon find ourselves not only in the higher overtones of the fourth dimension, which is the first step, but far beyond. We will continue to move up through the dimensional levels until at some point, soon, we will move through the great wall and into the next octave. This is a totally unheard-of event in the history of our universe.

There also appears to be a resolution in progress to the age-old question of Lucifer versus the light. God planted a seed and created a situation where it was the only choice. It came from technology onto a Lucifer rebellion planet (Earth). It now seems to be coming up with the answer for both sides.

Thanks to the dance between Archangels Lucifer and Michael, a situation was created, taking what had always been a very slow process into super acceleration. It is now beyond all the players; something greater than the created hierarchy has stepped forth and is expressing itself.

The trigger could have been the all-encompassing attention we have received. God created a situation so interesting that all life just had to look and, as we know, the observer affects the outcome of the experiment.

It appears that God (us on the other side of the waveform universe) has intervened directly. We are going back home!

Notes

1. Anthony R. Curtis, *The Space Almanac* (Woodshire, MD: Arcsoft Publishers, 1990), p. 607.

2. "Science News," Washington, DC: Science Service, Inc., Vol. 102, No. 8, August 19, 1972, p. 119.

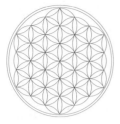

15

The Secret Government

Whether you call them the secret government, the Illuminati, the Bilderbergers, the Trilateral Commission, or the Council on Foreign Relations, the name is irrelevant. The "secret government" is basically made up of the richest people in the world. There are about 2,000 of them and they have been controlling our so-called governments for a long time. They control who gets elected, when, and where; they control when there is a war and when there isn't. They control planetary food shortages and whether a country's currency is inflated or deflated. All these things are dominated completely by these people. They can't control natural disasters, of course, but they can and do control a lot.

Somewhere between 1900 and 1930, the Greys made contact with these people. It was obviously well before 1943 because, in the Philadelphia invisibility experiment, scientists used information they had gotten from the Greys. Nikola Tesla, a physicist who for a time was the director of the Philadelphia Experiment, stated for the record that he was getting information from ETs, although no one believed him at the time.[1]

In the beginning, the secret government thought the Greys were benevolent and made an agreement with them. In fact,

they thought the Greys were the best thing that ever came along, a new source of limitless power. The agreement gave the Greys the right to experiment on the planet in exchange for their technology. It is this technology that has resulted in the incredible advancements we have made.

In 1968, when David Suzuki predicted that we would soon have a new north and south pole and that it would demolish just about everything on the planet, the secret government decided to leave. By 1970 they fused the Soviet Union and the United States; what is now happening, as we leave the Cold War behind us, was inevitable because we have been functioning as one country for a long time.

The secret government has never shared the Greys' technology with humanity at large but kept it for themselves. They have become so far advanced technologically it would be very hard for us to believe. They have had UFOs for a long time and they are way beyond that. It has been estimated that about 50 percent of the UFOs sighted are our own.[2] These craft are not extraterrestrial but belong to the secret government. They took Soviet, American, and Grey technology and created vehicles to make sure that they could get out of here before the shift. They began to prepare very rapidly; they knew they didn't have much time, only about fourteen years according to Suzuki's prediction.

First they made a base on the Moon, using it as a satellite to go deeper into space. They built three small bubble-type cities on the dark side. There was an accident on one of these and many people were killed. Records will indicate that there have been more than 2,000 secret missions to the Moon.

Once this secret government program got enough materials on the Moon they went into deeper space, and where do you think they went? Mars, of course, the ancestral home of the Greys. On Mars they built an extremely complex underground city designed to hold them and a few more people. Not many more, though; their main concern was saving themselves and they didn't much care about anyone else. This has been their style all along. They have become much like the Greys and have lost most of their emotional bodies. They brought to their colony on Mars everything they thought they would ever need.

According to Al Bielek, who worked on the Montauk (officially the Phoenix) Project:

> One of the uses of the Phoenix Project, in the use of Time Tunnels, was to provide backup to the Martian Colonies. The Martian Colonies have been there since the early '70s. We went publicly to the moon in 1969. Actually the Germans were there in 1947. And we were there in 1962 with a joint U.S.-Russian expedition. They went to Mars on May 22, 1962. The movie, *Alternative 3,* done by Anglia Television, April 1, 1977, which is available in the underground, outlines it completely. It shows the actual transmission—the color shots by TV back from Mars, as this Explorer moved and landed. We have colonies there in Mars from the late '60s or maybe early '70s onward.[3]

At that time not only did they not want anyone to know what they were doing, but they didn't want anyone to compete technologically with them either. Anyone who was involved in advanced technology was stopped in one way or another (as with a gag order). If they couldn't stop them they just got rid of them.

Somewhere around 1984 the secret government's city on Mars was completed. They began thinking that they really had it made. Then just a few years ago—approximately 1989 but Drunvalo doesn't know the exact date—they made a shocking discovery. The Earth is not the only place that the north and south pole are shifting; it is happening on all the planets in our solar system including Mars.

Seven to nine months later a further blow hit when they learned that it wasn't just a physical change that was occurring but also an interdimensional change in consciousness. At that point, like the Greys, they felt quite helpless because there wasn't much they could do. They then realized the only way they could survive was through love and unity consciousness.

This was the situation the Earth was faced with in Atlantis and ignored 16,000 years ago when the Martians tried to split off from the rest of the Earth's population and go their own way. The members of our secret government now know they can't survive on their own. They are leaving people like Drunvalo alone, people who might have an answer and might be able to help them.

Let's go back for a moment to Richard Hoagland and his research on the monuments of Mars. NASA's curious lack of involvement in Hoagland's research is precisely because Mars is the wrong planet for us to be examining. There is a lot happening on Mars that they don't want us to know about. NASA has tried everything it can to ridicule the information on the monuments so as to distract attention.

Insofar as these people are totally aligned with the Greys, they are pretty much devoid of emotions; however, they are extremely intelligent. If they could figure out any other way to save themselves they probably would, but they are now realizing from life forms much higher than the Greys that if they are to survive we all must—we are all in this thing together.

This is what the higher beings have wanted since the disaster in Atlantis. They didn't want just the Earthlings to survive at the expense of the Martians or vice versa; they wanted them both to survive and to go from there.

Notes

1. Preston B. Nichols and Peter Moon, *The Montauk Project: Experiments In Time* (New York: Sky Books, 1992), Appendix E.

2. Gordon-Michael Scallion, "UFOs From Earth," *Earth Changes Report* (Westmoreland, NH: The Matrix Institute, Vol. 2.4, May 1, 1992).

3. Al Bielek, quoted from an interview by Susanne Konicov, *The Connecting Link* (Grand Rapids, MI: Susanne Konicov, Issue 19).

* Further resources for this chapter were *Science Report,* "Alternative 3," from a broadcast of Anglia Television Limited, Norwich, England, April 1, 1977, Anglia Productions, written by David Ambrose, produced by John Rosenber; and Milton William Cooper, "The Secret Government, The Origin, Identity, and Purpose of MJ-12" (Huntington Beach, CA: Manuscript copyright 1989).

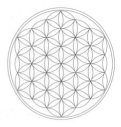

16

What Usually Happens

Drunvalo doesn't know what will happen when the pole shift takes place this time, and probably no one else does either because what we are doing is so unusual. Thoth and the other ascended masters believe, however, that we will have a much more gentle, organic, and conscious ride from one dimension to the next than is usually the case.

Drunvalo does know what usually happens when a pole shift takes place. When we approach the point in the precession of the equinoxes where the change takes place, everything begins to break down.

The key is the magnetic field of the Earth, which is what we use to interpret who and what we think we are and also to store our memory. We are very much like a computer in this sense. We need some form of magnetic field to process data.

The day before, the day of, and the day after the full moon there is usually an increase in murder, rape, and other crimes because the moon causes a bubble on the magnetic field. This minute bubble is enough to push already emotionally disturbed people over the edge.

As the shift approaches, things start to get out of balance and the magnetic field begins to fluctuate significantly over a very short period of time (about three to six months). This would be like a full moon getting bigger and brighter every day. What happens then is that people start to go crazy emotionally. This breaks down economic and social structures on the planet because it is only people who keep these structures together. When they lose control everything else falls apart.

This may not happen this time. We may be able to keep the magnetic field together.

Usually the pole and dimensional shifts are simultaneous. About five to six hours before the actual shift happens an extraordinary visual phenomenon takes place. The third and fourth dimensions actually begin to interface. Third-dimensional consciousness gradually recedes away from us as we approach fourth-dimensional consciousness.

As the third-dimensional grid begins to break down, synthetic objects disappear. This is one reason that even though there is a 500-million-year history of advanced life on this planet, there is virtually no evidence of it. In order to survive pole shifts, objects must be made purely out of natural materials like the pyramids and the Sphinx, natural materials that are in resonance with the Earth. Even then virtually everything on the planet is literally blown away.

As the synthetic objects begin to disappear, fourth-dimensional objects may suddenly emerge. Colors and shapes unlike anything we have ever known will appear on the landscape.

In order to consciously move from the third to the fourth dimension it has usually been necessary to create a merkaba, but this time may be a little different. According to Drunvalo we have already reached the point where 1½ billion people will definitely make the conscious shift, and the masters are projecting that everyone or almost everyone will make it into the next dimension. People may just all of a sudden know or remember the merkaba even though they won't remember how they knew it.

Even if we are able to keep the magnetic field together up until the actual shift, there will almost certainly be a three-and-a-half-day period when it will be completely gone. If you can manifest a merkaba, you have your own living time-space vehicle around your body first of all to replace the magnetic field that has collapsed, and secondly to travel from one dimension to the next.

As soon as the magnetic field collapses, the Earth will disappear for you and you will be in the Great Void. The duration of this "bardo" is three and a half days. Then life will come back in the fourth-dimensional world.

You will find yourself in a brand new world the likes of which you have never conceived. You have been there many times before, but your memory of it has been erased. You will be just like a baby, having no idea what all the colors and objects are.

One similarity between this world and the next is the Holy Trinity—that is, the mother, father, and child. As you enter this new world, though you understand nothing, you will be greeted by two beings, one male and one female, father and mother. You will have a very close love connection to these beings. When you enter the fourth dimension it will take about two years experientially to grow and mature. The growth is literal, by the way, given that the height range on this level is from ten to sixteen feet. Your new parents will guide and assist you during your growth.

You will appear just as you are now though more than likely naked. Clothing usually doesn't make it through. However, the atomic structure of your body, though it comes through, will have changed dramatically. The mass of your atoms will have been converted to energy. The individual atoms will have separated from one another at phenomenal distances. Most of your body will be energy, a light body. Remember, in this new world you will be creating your reality moment by moment with your thoughts. Manifestation will be instant: if you think "orange," an orange will instantly appear and you can peel and eat it.

This is why thoughts like peace, beauty, love, and so on are so important. If you are motivated by fear in the fourth dimension you will create and manifest your reality instantly, and you will instantly find yourself confronted by something terrifying like an antagonist trying to murder you. Then you will instantly manifest a gun and shoot them, and when that happens you will be bounced right back down to the third dimension where the link between cause and effect is slower. The quality of thoughts is totally important on the fourth dimension. This is what Jesus meant when he stressed the purity of thoughts. Love and peace and unity and being kind to your neighbors are ultimately very practical because they work reciprocally.

These things are important on the third dimension also, but, because of the time delay in manifestation, we get away with playing dumb and not seeing cause and effect. The third dimension seems to be a realm for mastering limitations or victim consciousness. In victim consciousness, the ultimate victim is one who doesn't know that he or she is creating reality, and believes that things just happen to them.

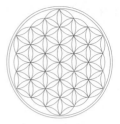

17

Rebirthing

Rebirthing is a tool that enables you to directly experience the One Spirit that moves through everything. Not only that, rebirthing teaches in a way that allows you to create for yourself an inner experience of unity as an ongoing process.

The only way to unite with the Spirit is to discover it within. This is the *only* way, and in so doing you're uniting with the infinite power of the universe.

Rebirthing is about learning how to breathe energy with air. It is the same energy that built and maintains your body; it is life-force energy or prana. It is thoroughly capable of cleansing, balancing, and healing your body.

Rebirthing is much more than just breathing; it is a combination of consciously breathing energy along with correctly using your mind so that you bring the two into harmony, working in alignment with each other.

The practice we are talking about here is rhythmic breaths in which "inhale" and "exhale" are connected without any pause in between them. The emphasis is on the inhale; the exhale is totally relaxed. This type of breathing will facilitate the movement of energy in your body—very pure, very powerful light energy, the energy of the life force itself. The natural tendency of this energy is to bring to your attention anything that you are holding on to that is less pure than itself.

Again, rebirthing is much more than just breathing. The process also includes expanding your ability to relax into, tune into, feel, and be at peace with whatever is going on in your body. This results in emotional resolution. The focus is on expanding to include all the physical sensations in your body, ranging from emotions (which do feel like something) to tingling, vibrating, and the like. These sensations will then gradually integrate into your greater sense of well-being. This enables you to let go of negativity you have been carrying around as a result of suppressing emotions.

Rebirthing is about completing the past. Incompletions from the past live in the body, absolutely, totally, and completely in the form of what you might call stuck energy, held in place by shallow breathing. To those of you who have done any bodywork, it might be obvious what I am talking about here.

Contrast rebirthing with the ways in which you might have dealt with unwanted emotions in the past. Let's take anger, for example. First, it is almost certainly not present-time anger, but most likely is an incompletion from the past being triggered by a present-time experience. This is how incompletions from the past work; they continue to manifest in present time and we usually resist. Around and around it goes. One way people deal with anger is to internalize it by denying it, suppressing it, or blaming oneself. Another way is to externalize it by blaming others, kicking and screaming, or acting it out in some other way. Neither way ever produces emotional resolution.

What works is to apply the process of rebirthing, that is, connected breathing, relaxing into the feeling, feeling it in exquisite detail, and continuing to make peace with what you are feeling.

Working at the feeling level is faster and much more direct than working directly with the mind. You do not need to have a cognitive understanding of what is happening. You can do it entirely at the level of sensation. That alone will change how your mind relates to the situation.

Fundamental to expanding your ability to relax into and feel bodily sensations is the context in which you are holding your experiences. At the very least you need to be willing for sensations to be the way they are, even if you don't like them. This *will* work. Even more useful, however, is the willingness to hold everything you are feeling as a healing in process. By relaxing into and allowing your feelings on the deepest level you will create your own healing. Ultimately, this will lead you to a feeling of gratitude for things being just the way they are.

Keep in mind that the natural function of energy as it moves through your body is to bring to your attention whatever you have been suppressing or holding on to. That's just its physics, how it works. Thankfully, it does this a layer at a time—you do not get more than you can handle. A layer at a time, breath by breath, emotions or feelings that you have been avoiding are brought to your attention by the moving energy. "Avoiding" here implies that you have been judging that there is something about these emotions or feelings that is "wrong."

I want to lump a few terms together: make-wrong, judgment, and resistance. When I use one term I am generally connoting them all. So whenever you are judging something or making something wrong, what you are doing in effect is locking the energy in place. What is fundamentally important here is the willingness to change your mind about whatever it is you have been making wrong.

A rebirthing session operates in a setting of safety and trust, and this environment gives you an expanded ability to be with and relax into physical and emotional sensations and, in so doing, begin the process of their completion. Shifting to a positive context gives you an expanded ability to allow things to be the way they are, rather than resisting them. Whatever you and I resist not only persists but, in direct response to our resistance, also gets stronger. If we find a particular mood or sensation uncomfortable and avoid it, then its demands on us become stronger and harder to evade. We are giving it energy by resisting it. If you are breathing against resistance it is going to get magnified and multiplied. The very things you are avoiding almost magically confront you again and again at every turn. On the other hand, you can easily and effortlessly move through the same material and dissolve it by going with it.

When you are breathing energy and relaxing into and tuning into the sensations you are feeling in your body and allowing them to be the way they are, the healing process begins. This can be easy, pleasurable, and even blissful.

Now, having said all this, perhaps the most important point is that none of this has to be taken literally, none of it is chiseled in stone. The key factor, the most important aspect, is your willingness to participate in the process in the first place. Included here is the willingness to let go of whatever you have been holding on to and to feel that peace and happiness are more important for you than being right or getting even. This willingness is what allows everything else to happen. With this volition, you do not have to do anything else perfectly, and the session will be effective.

The most important factor, whether practicing how to ride a bike or learning to breathe energy, is your willingness to do it in the first place and your commitment to it. If that willingness and that commitment are rock-solid, you will learn, and everything that happens will contribute to the completion of the process. That willingness alone gives you enormous freedom to just *be*. The freedom leads you to an expanded ability to relax and let energy flow.

In order to have a direct experience of the unity of being, you have to expand to include all of yourself. In other words, the habit of compartmentalizing yourself is a direct offshoot of duality, of creating your source externally as opposed to internally. The fragmentary parts of ourselves—incompletions from the past, things we are too fearful to be with—we tend to compartmentalize. We think we are putting them away, burying them so we won't have to deal with them. But this is fundamentally holding part of ourselves as shameful or wrong, and that part will always be exposed as less pure by the breath.

There is no possible way to experience unity of being when you are holding your life, your being, like this. Expanding your ability to accept the underlying safety and trust of the universe in the setting of a rebirthing session gives you an expanded ability to be with those things you have been resisting. As you experience them in this way, they begin literally to dissolve, and when they dissolve your duality begins to dissolve also. That is, events arise and dissolve in breath. It matters little whether the events are childhood, birth, past life, or whatever you consider them to be. It matters only that there is stuck energy that is dissolving. What you are left with is the unity of being as a living presence within you. You have a direct— not a theoretical—experience of the living spirit in your body.

This is equivalent to saying there is integration of both sides of the brain. The conceptual male side fuses with the female intuitive side.

I emphasize that this is not a regressive process to take you back to birth, early childhood, and so on, even though memories of these experiences may come up for you in a session. What alone matters about these incompletions from the past is to discover what you are currently carrying with you in a way that continues to manifest in present time. Your best access to these feelings is in present time. What you are carrying with you in the form of stuck energy definitely feels like something, and you can access it in that way.

The process then is about breathing, relaxing, tuning into feelings, and shifting the way you have been habitually holding them in avoidance, resistance, and making wrong. The process is about expanding your identity breath by breath to include these feelings so that they can integrate into a greater sense of well-being. In doing so, the past begins to complete itself.

Learning to rebirth yourself from a professional rebirther gives you a tool that you can use anytime to spark emotional resolution and the experience of the unity of being.

Over time you will learn to rely on your own authority rather than external authority. You will learn how the source is within, not without.

The teacher is the breath itself. It unfolds to you at its own rate. It moves at the rate that is perfect for you, which is never the same for any two people. Your breath is the vehicle to take you to your own source, the higher self that resides within you.

In addition to being the direct connection to your higher self, rebirthing has many additional advantages: 1) Your breath is readily accessible to you. 2) When you have the ability to breathe prana, it becomes easy to release any physical symptoms or negative thoughts. 3) It is safe. Breathing and relaxing can never hurt you. 4) It is a kinesthetic process (which means that the focus is on integrating into your sense of well-being *all* sensations/feelings in your body). Kinesthetic processing is faster and more direct. A single feeling can be worth thousands of words and concepts that would take hours to talk about. You can rationalize many situations in your mind, and your mind can keep you in denial for years.

Your body doesn't lie. Feelings are much harder to deny, and feelings let you know the results of your unconscious and conscious thoughts immediately. 5) Rebirthing can be used to enhance any other self-improvement technique, therapy, or treatment.

Twenty Connected Breaths

The foundation of rebirthing is a simple exercise that I learned from Leonard Orr, called twenty connected breaths.

You can do this exercise throughout the day, whenever you feel the need. However, it is recommended that for the first week you only do it once daily:

1. Take four short breaths.
2. Then take one long breath.
3. Pull the breaths in and out through your nose.
4. Do four sets of the five breaths, that is, four sets of four short breaths followed by one long breath without stopping, for a total of twenty breaths.

Merge the inhale with the exhale so the breath is connected without any pauses. One inhale connected to one exhale equals one breath. All twenty breaths are connected in this manner so you have one series of twenty connected breaths with no pauses.

Consciously pull the inhale in a relaxed manner and let go completely on the exhale while continuing to keep the inhale and exhale the same length.

Use the short breaths to emphasize the connecting and merging of the inhale and the exhale into unbroken circles.

Use the long breath to fill your lungs as completely as you comfortably can on the inhale, and to let go completely on the exhale.

Breathe at a speed that feels natural for you. It is important that the breathing be free and natural and rhythmical, rather than forced or controlled. This is what enables you to breathe prana as well as air.

Since most of us have developed bad breathing habits you might experience some physical sensations, such as lightheadedness or tingling sensations in your hands or elsewhere. If you do this exercise daily, you will notice that the sensations may change and become less overwhelming, and more generative of healing. This indicates that you are learning about breathing consciously and are getting direct benefits in your body.

Daily practice of this exercise will teach you more about breathing than you have ever learned in your entire life.

If you wish to accelerate the process, contact a professional rebirther and schedule a series of one- to two-hour guided sessions.

The majority of people take from two to ten sessions to feel safe, trust the process, and develop their skills of breathing, relaxing, focusing, and finding positive contexts. A professional rebirther has experienced the energy sensations that come up during a breathing session and has knowledge of how to adjust the breath and how to create a setting of total safety with regard to those sensations. A good rebirther is only a breathing guide who allows and trusts *your own* life energy to do the session. In truth, you control the session. Rebirthers create an environment of safety for you to experience your own divine energy and bliss. A good rebirther will also give you tools to help you unravel your own birth/death cycle. Some rebirthers can telepathically pick up what the energy is doing in your body and channel energy to make your session more powerful. However, the main goal of the rebirther is to teach you how to rebirth yourself.

Therefore, it is very important to choose a professional

rebirther that you feel comfortable with, and you have confidence in their teaching skills. Please be aware that the name "rebirthing" is not trademarked, and there are individuals out there who call themselves rebirthers teaching people to scream, cry, and pound pillows. Rebirthing is about *BREATHING* and *BEING* with all your feelings, not acting them out. It is learning to breathe prana and to be aware of the energy in your body, as well as unraveling the birth/death cycle.

If you would like to learn from me, in addition to private sessions I also offer my three-day workshop "Nothing to Something" (The Sacred Science of Rebirthing).

In the workshop, along with a thorough teaching of the fundamentals, you will receive two rebirthing sessions. This all happens in a setting of awareness, understanding, safety, and trust.

"Nothing to Something" continues where the "Flower of Life" leaves off, and proceeds to show you in a more right-brained, experiential way the actual process of moving from polarity into unity consciousness.

You are also shown the single most important aspect of keeping your merkaba field balanced and stable—the process of emotional body clearing, which teaches you how to consciously move through your fears and limitations, and how to move *with* the tremendous changes that we are all experiencing.

But "Nothing to Something" is much more than that. It is about reclaiming your personal power in ways you probably never thought possible. It is about discovering that you have everything you need, and it is all self-contained.

Each workshop is complete in its own right, however, it takes both to fully paint the bigger picture and to show how to step into the larger reality of our true nature, so we can consciously take control of our own destiny. The two are like holograms, meaning that each contains the whole. However, the "Flower of Life" goes into detail in areas that we only touch on in "Nothing to Something" and vice versa.

Both come from the ground of being that you are a spiritual master having a human experience, and your true purpose is to co-create heaven on Earth. The workshops can be taken in either order.

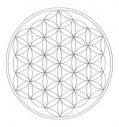

18

Your Body Is Light and
You Are Immortal

I first heard the idea of physical immortality in March 1979, when I was introduced to rebirthing. It sounded like the weirdest thing I had ever heard; it just did not compute. The notion crashed headlong into my unexamined and unquestioned belief that death is inevitable and totally beyond my control. I even reacted to it with anger: "What kind of New Age malarkey are they trying to sell me now?"

Not long after I met Leonard Orr. He talked about physical immortality all the time; he was even writing a book on the subject.[1] It didn't sound as weird to me this time around; in fact, I was beginning to like the idea, especially once I came to realize that it was really about the *quality* of life right here and now. After all, if you are miserable, why would you want to continue the misery any longer than necessary? On the other hand, if the quality of your life is great and getting better all the time, maybe you wouldn't mind sticking around a little longer.

Let's go back to birth in order to see if we can get a handle on what happens to us. At birth, if the cord is cut prematurely, we are not given an opportunity to learn how to

197

breathe in a relaxed, safe environment. Breathing is forced upon us in a do-or-die situation. We learn to breathe in a setting of fear and tension. From our first forced breath at birth, full free breathing becomes subconsciously equated with pain and fear, so we learn to breathe shallowly. This shallow breathing becomes the equivalent of holding a lid on a pressure cooker. All that urgency then gets compacted into our breathing mechanism and literally lives in our body, in a suppressed state, in the form of blocked or stuck energy. This stuck energy is statically held in place by shallow breathing.

Since there is no outlet for the "steam"—the stuck energy—it continues to build and the body becomes an increasingly unpleasant place to live in. We withdraw our awareness from it. Physical death is the ultimate form of withdrawn bodily awareness.

Just imagine if you lived in a house that you had not cleaned for thirty or forty years—you probably wouldn't want to spend much time there. It is the same with your body.

So the idea of physical immortality is really about the quality of life here and now. It is also an idea that allows rebirthing to proceed more effectively, by enabling you to create a context that is inclusive of any and all of your limiting and fearful thoughts.

Leonard used to talk about some of the people who had written about physical immortality and how most of them had since died. No big surprise, right? He even mentioned one person who died while on his way to give a talk on the subject. Leonard learned not to trust these people.

He developed a new set of criteria. He decided he would not believe anyone who talked about immortality unless they were at least 300 years of age!

In the late 1970s he traveled to India where he met Babaji, an immortal yogi master. He has since met seven or eight individuals in India who are at least 300 years old. From these actual living examples, he learned the common denominators, the secrets of maintaining a physical body beyond the "normal" lifespan. They all are rooted in increasing the quality of aliveness.

As you might suspect, it all begins with the knowledge of the energy body. Earth, air, water, and fire can clean the mind more efficiently than the mind can clean itself. The conscious use of these cleanses and balances the energy body.

The idea, then, is to use the elements first to clean out our accumulation of toxins, fears, and tensions, and then to stay ahead of the pollution process.

Earth purification means developing a conscious relationship to your body, and to the environment and planet. It has to do with food mastery, movement or exercise, and experiencing nature directly to the point where you can feel the immediate results of being in the woods or by a stream.

Air purification is breathing consciously, breathing energy or prana as well as air.

Water purification is bathing consciously so you can learn actually to feel and appreciate what the water is doing for you. The purpose of conscious bathing is to clean and balance the energy body.

Fire purification is sitting by a fire so your energy body or wheels of energy can turn through the flames. It is learning through personal experience what it feels like to have your energy body or aura directly cleansed by fire.

These are some of the common practices shared by actual immortals living on the planet today. And they also practice the continual remembrance of God, the One and eternal Spirit that moves through everyone and everything.

If you put these methods into practice, you will begin to discover that you are more than just a physical body. You will discover that you are an energy body, too. You will also tap the enormous practical value of working with the energy body directly.

Does this mean you will live forever in your current body if you start practicing these techniques? Probably not. But it does mean that you can learn to rejuvenate and revitalize and heal yourself. And can you even learn how to reverse the aging process? Absolutely!

Remember too, that as Drunvalo says, immortality is not about living forever in a body—that is a trap. There is always a higher reality to evolve into. Immortality is about consciously leaving when you want to, and retaining your memory as you ascend through the heights. It is about remembering who you are, always.

Notes

1. Leonard Orr, *Physical Immortality, The Science of Everlasting Life* (Sierraville, CA: Inspiration University, 1980).

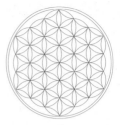

19

Rebirthing:
The Left Eye of Horus

Rebirthing is emotional body training. It is a modern-day equivalent of the Left Eye of Horus, dealing directly with fears, feelings, and emotions and enabling you to integrate them into your greater sense of well-being.

It is interesting, and probably no coincidence, that I had had almost exactly twelve years of emotional body training (rebirthing) before I discovered the missing material, the Right Eye of Horus, and the rest of Drunvalo's information.

Rebirthing quickly opened me up to the realization of how much I had been living in my head, living life conceptually and not even noticing it. I was not in my body and did-n't realize it. I had no frame of reference. I didn't know, and I didn't know that I didn't know. I was asleep and blind.

The most important thing I learned from rebirthing was that integration, healing, or completion (I use these three terms interchangeably) come from taking responsibility for one's life. There must be a willingness to confront and accept whatever it is that you have been avoiding or resisting. Remember, whatever we resist not only persists, it actually becomes more intense the more we resist it. True healing emerges from expanding your ability to include, be with, and ultimately embrace what you have been resisting.

Integration is not about denial or avoidance, nor is it about "positive thinking." It is about having both eyes open and being aware of polarities and emotions that have been running your life. Once something integrates, you have a greatly expanded ability to be with things as they are, rather than seeing them through your fears, doubts, or anger.

I recall how I was at the mercy of my emotions, how easily and often instantly I could be devastated, depressed, or angered by others' actions. Other people seemed to have control over me—they "made" me happy or sad or angry or whatever. This was my reality. I was not the source of my experience in life, others were.

I first heard of the notion that I create my own reality and am responsible for it in the est training in 1977. It was a powerful and profound experience. I essentially only learned it as a concept, however.

I began to understand the idea of responsibility more fully through rebirthing. As I came into the living presence of emotions, feelings, and beliefs that were running me, I slowly began to realize that I would never achieve resolution until I began to own what was going on with me.

A major impediment at the time was a debilitating lower back injury, for which I was taking no responsibility. It was something that had "happened to me." I felt completely victimized by it. I was certain it was not curable and would only get worse, and I would soon be completely crippled by it.

I had certain "pay-offs" from my back injury, though. It gave me a great opportunity to be helpless. Early in life I learned the benefits of helplessness—how I got waited on, attended to, and cared for much better whenever I was sick. I was too often taken for granted or even ignored when I was well, so being "helpless" was better.

I had a lot of emotional baggage connected with my back injury, and it was all literally living in the injured area to the point where I felt as though my body were severed in two, as if all the life energy had left that area of my body.

It gradually dawned on me that, like it or not, the only way out was to begin to own my life and what was going on with me.

So I did. I began to accept the idea that I created my back injury and everything else in my life. As I did this, I began to let go of the superficial "pay-offs" one by one, reclaim my own personal power, and move towards healing.

I have long since healed my back to the point where it feels as though it was never crippled. I also no longer am emotionally manipulable by other people to the degree I once was.

I also used rebirthing to come to terms with many other fears that were limiting me. For example, I had some very intense fears of driving stemming from childhood experiences. I learned them from my father as he had learned them from his father. He never sat me down and explained directly to me how fearful driving was to him; he didn't have to—I learned this every time we got in the car to go somewhere. The most memorable lessons came from our frequent trips to visit my grandparents, a distance of about 180 miles. It was bad enough under normal road conditions, but you can imagine the icy and snowy weather that always seemed to await us during Thanksgiving and Christmas in North Dakota.

It was awful—in fact, it was worse than that. The fear and tension were thicker than pea soup or London fog, take your pick.

In order to alleviate his fears, my father would smoke in the car. I enjoyed that so much I would usually show my appreciation by getting car-sick. This was my contribution.

Of course when I grew up I became a licensed driver. I recall my first solo trip, and even though it was less than one mile through town on empty streets, I was so nervous and scared that I don't know how I made it. By some miracle I forgot to lock the keys in the car, and I even made it back home.

I gradually learned to suppress many of my fears and became a tolerable driver. But those fears were still inside me, and even though I was usually able to keep them at a less than conscious level, they would on occasion surface, as when I ran into some real traffic for the first time on an eight-lane highway between Sacramento and San Francisco while moving to California. I was a mess!

Rebirthing enabled me to integrate those fears, and I have long since become an excellent driver. I am extremely alert and aware of the traffic flow at all times, and I feel totally safe. I am able to be in the present moment with the experience of driving as it actually is, both eyes open, aware of potential danger.

This is not to say that I no longer experience fear or other so-called negative emotions. I do. The main thing is that I have a very different relationship to them now. I interact with them as if they are there for my benefit rather than something to be avoided or resisted. When I feel them, I breathe into them and release their energy into myself.

That in turn greatly enhances my ability to go into other feelings and get whatever message there is for me. Altogether this reinforces the idea that all is well and that my life is unfolding exactly as it should. Unity consciousness is my ever-increasing reality.

So what does this all mean? It means that I am no longer at the total effect of my emotions. It doesn't mean that I never feel stress; I do—that is part of our modern-day culture. But I do have the ability, using this tool called rebirthing, to cleanse, balance, and heal myself on a daily basis. The effects are powerful and profound. And if I can do it, anyone can. I am just an ordinary person.

The feeling after a completed energy cycle is incomparable. To experience your full aliveness and to be fully in your body is exhilarating! To me it is proof that this life was meant to work. All we have to do is align with it.

So I handled my fear of driving and sourced my emotions, so what? No big deal. That was all minor compared to the big event that came up for me, beginning in 1980.

I first heard about the Earth change prophecies in 1980 when I was in training to become a rebirther. However, I was too immersed in my own survival at the time to pay much attention.

My first real lesson came during Christmas 1981 when Leonard Orr gave an evening seminar at Theta House, a rebirthing center in San Francisco. He passed out a short essay entitled "The Rebirth of the Late, Great Planet Earth." It made for interesting reading. He spoke of Earth changes (earthquakes, floods, pole shifts, etc.), all happening in the very near future and taking up to 90 percent of the planet's population with them.

I could have dismissed all that as pure fantasy, but I didn't. First, I had a lot of trust and faith in Leonard, and second, I knew as early as the late sixties that we (the planet) were on a collision course for disaster. So I took the information seriously and was convinced to varying degrees that it was literally true.

This exposure to the "Earth change" prophecies began an intense period of activation that took a few months to integrate. By activation, I mean "terror." As the information did integrate I slowly began to realize that I could live with these prophecies and still feel safe to be alive. I also began to realize that integrating this material made me feel more grounded in my body and more able to live in present time. I discovered that my sense of safety came from an inner source. My essential being rode way above this, like a creature in the heavens, experiencing this incarnation as only one aspect of itself, totally prepared, totally safe. I then was able to launch the most successful phase of my career.

What became clear was that it was *my* fears about survival and being able to be fully alive and successful that had been activated as a result of being exposed to the "Earth change" prophecies. As my fears integrated, of course, I went deeper into my true self. There was still more to learn about these prophecies, but I wasn't aware of that part yet. At least I was free. Then I needed a few more "lessons."

The next episode occurred in 1986 when I saw an eight-hour video presentation by Ramtha entitled "Changes." I began thinking, "Not again!" and braced myself for the next round of information to hit.

It took a while, but as that integrated I found myself more grounded again, and very much more successful in my rebirthing practice. The larger lesson was beginning to take form.

Let it be said that in both of these Earth change scenarios, California was predicted to be drastically relocated—like to the bottom of the ocean. At the very least, California wasn't considered the ideal place to ride it all out.

Enter phase three. In April 1992 a new rebirthing client came to me. He saw a copy of a book on crop circles that I had and asked me about it. We talked about that for a while; then he asked if I had heard of Gordon-Michael Scallion. I had not, so he told me about him. Well, of course, this turned out to be more about Earth changes, much more. Scallion had been publishing a monthly paper called the *Earth Changes Report* in which he gave the most specific Earth change predictions yet and backed them up with an 87 percent accuracy rate. Among other things, he had accurately predicted the 7.1 Loma Prieta Earthquake near San Francisco in October 1989.

By the time we got around to the rebirthing session, the person who needed to be rebirthed was me. I was totally activated by this new information. It's funny looking back on it, but it wasn't funny at the time.

So there I went—into the pool to visit the crocodiles one more time. I still had not found the right way out. Of course, at the time I had not yet heard of the Left Eye of Horus, but I did know that the purpose of a prophet was to be wrong, that what a prophet does is give a wake-up call. If the prophet is successful we hear the call and the prophecy does not come true.

It is like the old Chinese proverb, "If we don't change our direction, we are likely to wind up where we are headed." And we are heading towards disaster; we have not been particularly conscious caretakers of spaceship Earth. I felt helpless back then, as though I had no choice in the matter. Whenever your fear or anger is sufficiently activated it does seem as though there is no choice because you are on full automatic. So back into the pool. In the moment of greatest fear, I had to learn to go deeper into my fears and helplessness. Of course I subscribed to Scallion's newsletter and received my monthly shock treatment.

In June of 1992 I saw Drunvalo's videos and everything began to make more sense. Drunvalo presented a much larger picture of what was happening; precession of the equinoxes, pole shifts, etc. These Earth changes all happened on a regular basis every 13,000 years, like clockwork, no big deal. It has been almost that long since the last pole shift, so we are due.

I also heard Drunvalo say that because of the Sirian intervention in 1972 and the incredible events that have since happened, we might have a gentler ride this time around. I heard the words, that is, but it didn't fully and finally integrate until April 1993.

For me, Drunvalo's material was the missing information. I had been committed to finding the missing links for some time; I had known that even though rebirthing was very powerful, I didn't have the bigger picture. If you could breathe a merkaba into being, why not breathe our passage between worlds? Why not everything? Up until this time I had been sitting mainly with the negative, dark side of the "Earth change" information. But who would fear a return to the Garden? An incomplete picture can be dangerous, especially if it is a dark one.

Finally, in April 1993 everything began to come together for me. Our reality and what happens to the Earth is a function of consciousness, so we do have the power to change the future. Knowing that, I decided to make it my personal business to ensure that our transition into the next dimension is a gentle one. I was finally waking up to my true purpose, what I was really here for—to be an interdimensional master co-creating heaven on Earth. So are you. It's just my job to remind you.

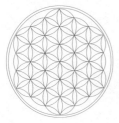

20

Healing

My first major lessons in healing came in the summer of 1980 when I was studying to become a rebirther.

I spent two months in Europe traveling and training with Leonard Orr, the founder. While in Europe I heard much talk of Babaji, the immortal yogi master referred to in Paramahansa Yogananda's book *Autobiography of a Yogi.*

I learned that Babaji had materialized a new adult body in 1970 and that he spent most of his time in his Herakhan ashram near the city of Haldwani in northern India. While in Europe I met quite a few people who had gone to India to find Babaji. They all had stories to tell, ranging from "just interesting" to "incredible."

One friend told of being caught in a rainstorm with Babaji. When they reached shelter, her clothes were soaked and Babaji's were completely dry, even though he was beside her in the same rainstorm.

I heard how he materialized his body out of a ball of light to Leonard and others outside of India, which inspired them to go to India to find him. I also heard that, to demonstrate his mastery of yoga, Babaji stayed in one position for forty-five days without moving. He sat motionless, no food, no water, nothing, for forty-five days (Fig. 20–1).

Figure 20–1. Babaji sat in this position without moving and
without food, for forty-five days.

I was also struck by a quote from Babaji: "If you come
to me with doubts, I will give you every reason to be doubt-
ful. If you come to me with love, I will show you more than
you have ever known." I knew it was important to remain

open to the possibility that Babaji was all that everyone said he was. I knew that if I closed myself down to that possibility, my experience would only be consistent with my doubts.

So I remained open. As a result I began to feel an increasing personal connection to him.

My entire European experience was a continual lesson of letting go and trusting. It began with having only enough money for a one-way ticket to London plus some loose change. That meant I had to earn my way as I went, teaching to others what I was learning myself, as I was learning it. That gave me a pretty fair idea of what it was like to be in the void. My old world had fallen apart and the new one was not fully in place yet.

I remember arriving in Stockholm, Sweden, with my traveling companion at two A.M. one morning. We knew no one and had nowhere to go, so we decided to find the site of the current rebirthing training that Leonard was leading. When we arrived there we saw a note on the front door telling us that no one was there, that the training had been moved to a farmhouse in the country many miles away.

There was literally no one there, then at three A.M. one person just happened to be walking by; she also spoke English. When we asked her if she knew of the whereabouts of the training, not only did she know, she gave us complete directions how to get there by bus, and she also let us sleep in her apartment that night.

I felt the presence of Babaji and knew that as long as I kept trusting and letting go, I would be safely guided to wherever I needed to be and whatever I needed to learn. I have had a personal relationship with Babaji ever since. I can feel his presence whenever I call upon it.

When I returned home from Europe, my cat Freddie, who was otherwise totally healthy, became paralyzed in the rear half of his body. He was not in pain but he had no use of his hind legs and could only move by inching himself forward with his front paws.

I took him to the veterinarian, who had no idea what the problem was and could offer nothing. I went into a funk over it, thinking how unfair it was. Freddie remained calm and peaceful and loving through it all and that almost made it worse for me.

Then I got a vision, a very clear vision that there was no reason at all, there was absolutely no reason at all that Freddie couldn't be perfectly healthy. The vision kept getting clearer and stronger until I saw and felt with total clarity and certainty that Freddie was normal and healthy.

Freddie began to heal, and in a short time was completely recovered and healthy. He never again showed any symptoms of paralysis.

Then one day Freddie came home with one eyelid shut. It remained that way for two or three weeks. When it finally opened it was one of the ugliest things I had ever seen. The eyeball looked like it was decayed to the point of no return.

I took him to the veterinarian, who gave him about a 10 percent chance of retaining his eyeball. He gave me some ointment and wished me luck. He also advised me of the importance of returning in a few days to have the eyeball removed.

Again, I began to have a clear vision of Freddie in perfect health! The vision intensified to the point where I saw it with absolute certainty and clarity. Freddie's eye immediately began to heal. It healed until there was no indication that anything had ever been wrong. I took him back to the veterinarian at that point for final confirmation. The vet could not believe it. He had never seen a healing like that before.

Throughout these two experiences, I knew intuitively that it was Babaji who was working through Freddie for the purpose of teaching me about healing. He was working through

Figure 20–2.

Freddie because at the time I had more love and compassion for my cats than I did for myself.

At the time I was half-crippled myself by my back injury, which Freddie was acting out for me. I was also convinced that I was helpless and powerless to heal myself and that it would only get worse. I could not have learned the lesson if it had been applied directly to me.

One day I was sitting in my room while looking at and meditating on a poster of Babaji (Fig. 20–2). Then a spontaneous voice inside of me asked, "Babaji, was it you?" The likeness of Babaji in the poster instantly became alive and animated. He smiled directly at me and nodded in the affirmative. I got the message.

From these experiences I learned a lot about healing. I learned the critical fact of coming from the heart.

I also learned the importance of breaking down prior belief systems and providing a willingness for healing to occur, and then being able to see it and feel it and know it with certainty.

As mentioned earlier, I have healed my back. I have also completely healed my breathing mechanism. For me, this was no small feat. As a child I had serious respiratory ailments including allergies, hay fever, and frequent colds.

I was diagnosed as being allergic to just about everything. I had hay fever that kept me in a constant state of misery in the spring and summer, and far too many colds would keep me in bed for periods from a few days to a few weeks.

That is now all history.

It is obvious to me that anything can be healed through the correct combination of thought, breath, and the heart.

Sickness is not something that just happens. It is the result of the improper use of breathing, thoughts, feelings, and actions.

Whatever your thoughts, feelings, and actions are in life creates your reality, including your health.

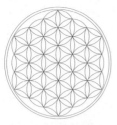

21

Life Context

When I talk about context, what do I mean? Let's first dis-
tinguish between context and content. Content is the thing
itself, and context is your relationship or attitude towards it.

In rebirthing, connected breathing allows suppressed
material to come to your attention, or to come into activation, so you can feel it. The reason the material was suppressed in the first place was that your relationship or attitude
towards it, or the context in which you were holding it, was
one of make-wrong. Otherwise you would not have been
suppressing it.

In the process of rebirthing you learn to shift your relationship to your suppressed material from make-wrong to
acceptance, or from a negative to a positive context. This
allows integration or completion to take place.

But at some point, larger make-wrongs, or negative judg-
ments about some aspect of yourself, will come to your attention. These harbor the conditions out of which the smaller
make-wrongs are generated. By a condition, I mean an unexamined, unquestioned, and unconscious structure of beliefs
that becomes the filter through which one unwittingly sees
life. We don't necessarily go around consciously thinking it,
but we live life out of that condition.

It is necessary at that point to have a context, a life con-text if you will, that is inclusive of that content. In the absence of such a context, that condition or set of beliefs becomes our unconscious life context.

Ultimately, it is necessary to have a life context large enough to include any limiting thought or condition that comes to your attention. This is the reason for knowing about angels, aliens, overtones, and Babaji. Within this context, the limiting thoughts and conditions become your allies. They are now arising within that larger context, in alignment with that context, and they get resolved as a result.

In the absence of that consciously created context, the very same material will come up in a way that serves always as evidence or proof of unworkability.

Mind Clearing 101

Remember, the basic principle is that when you create a life context, anything unlike it, or anything less pure than the context, is fair game to come to your attention. Only with breathing, it is arising now in a way that enables it to be resolved.

By analogy, let's suppose you have a glass of water, with a one-inch layer of mud on the bottom. If you run fresh clean water into the glass (life context) you immediately create a muddy mess (the subconscious impure thoughts that come to your attention). If you continue running clean fresh water into the glass, the mud will eventually get washed out, and you are left with a glass of fresh, clean water. The same is true regarding your mind, and I will give you two specific ways of doing this.

The first method is a way of using affirmations that takes advantage of this displacement principle. After you have written your affirmation, stop and notice if you have any response to it. If you do, write it down. Then write the affirmation again and continue the process until your responses begin to agree with the affirmation. This alignment will occur over a period of time, ranging from a few days to a few weeks.

Affirmation	Response
I am a master here to co-create heaven on Earth.	No way, you must be kidding.
I am a master here to co-create heaven on Earth.	Give me a break!
I am a master here to co-create heaven on Earth.	That's the dumbest thing I've ever heard.
I am a master here to co-create heaven on Earth.	Maybe it isn't quite the dumbest thing I've ever heard.
I am a master here to co-create heaven on Earth.	I wonder if it is possible.
I am a master here to co-create heaven on Earth.	Hmmm, I'll consider it.

Another method involves an exercise that was given to me by a friend and fellow rebirther by the name of Seth Bartlett, also known as Dhyana Yogi. It is called the Basic Thought Meditation.

The Basic Thought Meditation

1. Write down all your thoughts for five to ten minutes—every thought you remember long enough

to write. Don't censor anything, chase elusive
thoughts, or pursue lines of reasoning. Simply let
your mind flow onto the paper.

2. Read it over a few times and circle any phrase,
thought, or idea which "makes something wrong."
That is, circle any idea which indicates you are
thinking something is "not okay," "bad," or "wrong."
Example: Sam makes me mad.

3. On a separate page, one thought at a time, list the
positive opposite for each idea you circled. Use the
form: It's okay for _____ that _____.
Example: It's okay for *me to think* that *Sam makes
me mad.*

4. On another page, again one thought at a time,
develop a gratitude context for each idea you circled.
Use simple logic and the form: I'm grateful for
_____because _____. Example: I'm
grateful for *thinking that Sam makes me mad* because
*it is giving me an opportunity to take responsibility for
my own emotions.*

Helpful Hints

1. Developing a context for gratitude through logic is a
mental exercise. Do it mechanically. It is not
necessary to believe what you write or to actually
experience feelings of gratitude. Just write down any
context in which you see a logical basis for gratitude.

2. Look for the value in the situation, experience, or
whatever you are making wrong. When you look
deeply, you will always find some value.

3. Pretend that you personally ordered whatever you

are making wrong to be exactly the way it is, and then write down the reasons you want it that way.

4. Notice you are having certain feelings in your body. Assume you planned it exactly this way, and write down why you would do that. At the very least, you could be grateful for your ability to feel. Enthusiastically exaggerate the feeling it engenders to tense up your body to defend yourself against whatever you are making wrong. At this point, whatever you are experiencing may even be humorous.

5. Notice that whatever you are making wrong is not infinitely bad. You might be grateful that it's as good as it is.

6. Focus on your gratitude for being alive. See that whatever you are making wrong is part of being alive right now, and is exactly the way it is. It is a miracle that whatever you are making wrong even exists and that it happened at exactly the right time for you. Didn't it?

7. Stop comparing whatever you are making wrong to anything but itself. It could be interesting or even fascinating. Could it at least be intense? Pretend it's pleasurable, and open up to it.

8. Assume that whatever you are making wrong is a direct reflection of something you are making wrong about yourself. You could be grateful for noticing a way in which you make yourself wrong, especially if that awareness leads you to stop.

9. Be very loving, gentle, and patient with yourself. Give all parts of yourself unconditional love. Extend unconditional love to all aspects of your experience.

Who Am I?

What I managed to unravel through various disciplines and experiences were things that were keeping me from being fully alive. In fact, all that stuff "out there" (Earth change fears, environmental fears, secret government fears, etc.) was nothing but an external representation of my own inner state of affairs. This was the lens through which I was unwittingly seeing life.

In order to heal the fear, I needed to create enough trust and safety to fully experience it instead of being paralyzed by it. In other words, I had to have a context that was broad enough to include anything that might come to my attention, including death.

Immortalist philosophy begins by questioning whether or not death is inevitable and completely beyond your control. Just asking the question can be very empowering because it begins to lift you out of victim consciousness. After all, what better way to be a victim than to be immersed in the belief that you have no say in the fate of your physical body?

Remember, too, that whatever you believe to be true about your life you will unerringly create. In the meantime you will be less than fully alive because you will continue to suppress any thoughts or sensations associated with your unconscious and unquestioned beliefs about death.

Immortalist philosophy aids you in taking responsibility for these thoughts and feelings by providing a context that is broad enough to include them. They can then be resolved just like any other thoughts or feelings.

What made it tricky for me was the fear of global catastrophe. It might not be too great to still be around if everything were in ruins and up to 90 percent of the people were gone. On the other hand, it was the only problem big enough to fully engage me.

There was still something missing, and that is why I had a problem. I thought I had the ultimate context, but I came to realize that I didn't.

What was missing was the idea that our true nature is that of being interdimensional masters, that we exist on different dimensions simultaneously. In our higher aspects, then, we already are Christ-consciousness beings. We are spiritual beings having a human experience here in the third dimension. Having that awareness creates the possibility of living your life in its true context.

Our mission is to wake up to our true nature so we can get on with it, so we can do what we came here to do. Our true purpose is to bring our higher-dimensional light and wisdom here to co-create heaven on Earth, to assist the birth of this planet into the fourth dimension.

And the process is just like birth; in fact, it is birth. The more awake and conscious we are, the more we will be able gently and wisely to assist the planet. It can be a safe and exciting journey, but only if we say so.

Contrast that with the alternative. If we are asleep and filled with fear, then the birth will be a reflection of that— an experience filled with fear, pain, and struggle.

The entire planet, and everyone on it, is in the throes of this change. We are all mutating—the planet is in transition and so are we individually. Some of us are more conscious of this than others. It means we get to experience the joy of having more light flow through us and also the inconvenience of having our old world dissipate before the new one is completely together.

Like it or not, we are all mutating, and if we resist, it can get pretty tough. If you try to go back to your old way of being, it won't work anymore. If you begin to identify as a master here to co-create heaven on Earth you are moving in the direction of the transformation and therefore helping it. You will be able to find your way more easily.

We do create our reality unerringly. In fact, all we ever see "out there" is simply an outward reflection of our own inner state of affairs. If we see fear and limitation, it is because that is what is going on within us.

As we begin to wake up to our true nature and identify with the master that we are, this then becomes our inner experience. The more it becomes our inner experience, the more we are able to project it outside ourselves, and as we do this, we are indeed co-creating heaven on Earth. We do have the ability to change the future. It is all a function of our consciousness.

The second coming of Christ is not the second coming of a man; rather, it is an emanation of the luminescence within all beings who are ready. The beings on this planet are becoming illuminated from within, and they are beginning to rely more on their own internal authority. The Greys are gone; the balance is shifting.

As this happens, the planet has less work to do. At a certain point, an exponential level will be reached, the leap in dimensionality and consciousness will take place, and the planet will become lit from within.

We are not going to ascend and leave; we are going to ascend into light bodies and stay, but on the fourth dimensional level. Bon Voyage!

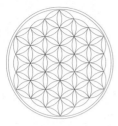

22

Completion

Ever since first viewing Drunvalo's videos, I had been planning to attend one of his workshops in person. I first contacted Drunvalo in February 1993 to ask his permission to use some of his material, and to be placed on his mailing list. He told me he would put me on the list, but I never heard from him. In fact, I heard nothing until December 1993 when my friend Alfred Lee informed me that Drunvalo would be giving a seminar in January 1994, the last "Flower of Life" workshop that he would give in person.

I decided to enroll along with my companion Lois and friend Alfred, but when I called to register I found that the seminar was filled. We were placed on the waiting list and told there was only a slim possibility we would get in, but were also informed that Drunvalo was considering giving one final workshop in April.

The January deadline came and passed with no word. Obviously we hadn't made it for the workshop, so I let it go and pretty much forgot about it.

Then one day in late February as I was thinking about calling Drunvalo to see about the next and final workshop, the phone rang. I answered; the person on the other end was Drunvalo Melchizedek. I was amazed at the "coincidence."

He told me he was indeed giving a final workshop in April in Austin, Texas, and that the "Flower of Life" portion had been expanded into six days, with three additional days of emotional body work designed to make firm contact with the higher self. He said there was room for Lois and me and wanted to know if we were interested.

Of course, I was interested. I immediately called Alfred to make sure he was also enrolled. Then I called my son Brett who, along with Lois and I, had attended the video workshop in June 1992, and had developed an interest in Drunvalo's work equal to mine. Brett was a third-year law student at the time and of course was very busy. He wasn't too busy for this, however, and he immediately confirmed that he wanted to take part in the workshop.

In our phone conversation Drunvalo also told me he was turning the workshop over to trained facilitators and that there would be a training program for those interested in becoming facilitators. This was the perfect complement to all my dreams and desires, the fulfillment of three years of intense searching.

In my years as a rebirther and seminar leader I had experienced a fair degree of success. In spite of this, I was becoming increasingly aware of what was *not* working.

The bottom line for me was struggle. I had plenty of emotional body training but was trusting it less because of the duality coming from my left brain. Also, I was becoming increasingly disillusioned with much of what I saw in the "New Age" movement. I saw more and more people who were talking about love and unity and acting "as if" life was wonderful, but who seemed totally ungrounded in reality. It was as though they had put on blinders to prevent themselves from seeing any negativity and in so doing, although they talked of unity, were in fact creating more separation.

I was also struggling with my rebirthing practice, which felt stale. It was becoming antiquated, out-dated; I kept trotting out the same old material and it just wasn't working as well anymore. It felt like rebirthing itself needed to be rebirthed. At least, my experience of it needed to be reborn.

So about three years ago (just about when this story began), I decided to let it all go as much as I could. I let most of my business go and I let go of struggle completely. I decided to do only what I wanted to do and to allow my logical left brain its full say—to expand enough to fully include all the duality and separation I saw until it fully integrated. Then and only then could I trust and believe the intuitive right side.

Our intuitive nature needs total support and confidence from our reasoning minds to remain grounded. It is the reasoning mind that needs to see the form behind all reality and that this underlying form totally connects everything. From this left-brained understanding, we are then able to open our hearts and feel the connection that our reasoning mind already knows without a doubt is there. Our reasoning minds can then fully support what we intuitively feel.

I now understand that this time in my life was about letting go of what wasn't working in order to create space for the *real* thing.

So we were off to Austin, Texas! I knew the workshop would be good, but I had no idea of what awaited me. It wasn't that I didn't know the material being presented— I was already intimately familiar with that, except for a small portion regarding Drunvalo's recent trip to England. But it was great hearing it presented in person and being able to ask questions; I gave my left brain full permission to ask every question I could think of and then some. Being able to ask questions was wonderful but that was just the beginning.

The experiential aspect of the workshop was absolutely incredible. As a group we created unity consciousness as a living presence; we were just different aspects of the whole—different cells in the one body. In essence, we created a fourth-dimensional reality.

It all began with Drunvalo, who I believe is the total embodiment of unity consciousness. He seems to always be in the present moment, living in the full awareness of his intimate connection with all life everywhere. He told us he would do his best to present the material and he kept his word. He was always fully available to anyone, and he never seemed to tire. He has the full aliveness, playfulness, and innocence of a child, yet is at all times in control of his material. He seems completely natural and nonjudgmental.

Truthfully, I've never seen anyone quite like him. For me, the most special thing about him is that he is here as a catalyst to show us that we all have this special quality: to see, live, and be the One Spirit in everyone and everything. Drunvalo emphasizes that we are all a part of God, that no one is better than anyone else. He presents himself not as a teacher, not a guru, but as a catalyst totally committed to demonstrating to *all* of us our own true nature.

At one point in the seminar we learned to see auras, by focusing our eyes differently, what you might call a "soft focus." We then trained this "soft focus" on a volunteer in white clothing who stood in front of a white background in dimmed light. The aura would then emanate around the person.

Drunvalo was the third and final volunteer. I saw his aura but what really struck me was his constantly changing facial image. It kept changing in rapid-fire succession as if there were three or four other entities present. I told him what I had seen and asked him about it. He said that the workshop was co-created by him along with Thoth and the four other Melchizedeks currently on the planet. He said that their energy is present and tends to surface when their areas of expertise are being discussed.

Then he went on to talk more about his walk-in experience. He told us that we were all quite likely walk-ins, and that the most likely time for the transfer was a near-death experience. When he said this it resonated in every cell of my body.

I immediately flashed back to a living death experience I had when I was in Amsterdam, Holland, in the summer of 1980.

This experience happened during my one-year training to become a rebirther. A very intense feeling had been coming on for a few weeks and it finally climaxed one evening. I could feel the life energy leaving my body just like air being let out of a balloon. My friends later told me that I became very pale. At the time, I felt I was standing outside of myself just witnessing the event. I experienced no fear; I didn't panic; I was just watching. I am certain that my belief in immortality kept me in total safety. After a few minutes, I came back into my body and discussed it with my friends, who had all witnessed the phenomenon as well.

Could this have been my walk-in experience? My memory of it resonated in me like it was true. I have learned to trust the messages my body sends me and this was one of the clearest signals I have ever received.

Drunvalo went on to say how as a walk-in you totally take on the karma of the body you inhabit and that you also get full use of its memory and training. Also, you will probably not consciously know you are a walk-in until the time is right. He then added that the time is now.

There is more than a fair chance that you too are a higher-dimensional walk-in, and that your reading this will serve as a catalyst to trigger your memory. If this is your truth, welcome!

I learned too, that like everything else, we exist in three-ness. We have a higher self, a middle self (ourselves in our bodies), and a lower self. In order to connect with the higher self, it is first necessary to connect with the lower self. There is no other way.

The lower self is our subconscious mind; it is a child, about two to six years old. You make connection with this lower self by learning to be child-like again, which means learning to be playful again. It also means being innocent, sensitive, and allowing your heart to open and reconnect with nature. We cannot connect with this lower self by approaching life as a sophisticated adult; it just doesn't work.

The lower self is not just our own subconscious mind; it is the subconscious mind of the entire planet with which we are connecting. We have lost this bond, we have severed our relationship with the Earth, and we very much need to re-connect.

Once you have connected with the lower self, you can make connection with the higher self. But you can't force it—it will happen only when the lower self knows you are ready, and it will then arrange it.

I realized that I was already very deeply into this process. It had begun in 1970 when I gave up my teaching career when I turned twenty-six and could no longer be drafted into the army. I was totally opposed to the Vietnam War and vowed not to participate. In 1970, I quit teaching in a system that I could see was not working, and decided to do only what I wanted to do and have fun.

Since 1970 I developed a wonderfully intimate connection with the elements and with the planet. They became totally alive for me and I love them dearly. However, I lost much of my playfulness and innocence, and this led directly to my decision three years ago when I had to just let go. I am now in the process of regaining these qualities.

I was very pleased to hear that Drunvalo had done exactly the same thing at pretty much the same time for similar reasons. He had done it perhaps more thoroughly, having moved to the woods to *really* reconnect with Earth.

During another guided process in the workshop, I met my higher self in the form of two angels—one female and one male. During this process I asked for "proof" that the connection was real. The "proof" came in the following way.

Drunvalo had mentioned earlier in the seminar that we would go into nature on the last day with the purpose of experiencing our interconnectedness with all life. He told us that we would be going to two very beautiful places. I was somewhat skeptical, as my concepts of Texas were of cattle and sagebrush and not much else. But I was wrong— we did go to two very beautiful, special places!

We first descended down a long, winding trail to a stream that led into a fairy-tale type setting: a pond with a semi-circular cavernous overhang, almost like a grand-stand carved out of the Earth. There we spent a couple of hours connecting with nature and doing the fourteen-breath meditation.

As we were leaving, I noticed some fish in the stream and kneeled down to have a better look. The water was calm and peaceful and I could clearly see the fish swimming around, totally unaware of my presence. Then one fish, about twice the size of the others, came swimming up as close to me as it possibly could and made direct eye contact. I knelt down even further to get as close to the water as I could. We were about three feet apart and maintained this direct contact for what seemed like several minutes. This fish had an intelligent "self-aware" presence about it, definitely different from the other fish, who were oblivious to the both of us. The fish then swam away a few feet but in a few seconds came back and re-established eye contact with me. This lasted at least two more minutes.

I have connected with wild animals before—squirrels, raccoons, foxes, and once I was able to approach and pet a deer. But I have never before connected with a fish. The experience was amazing; I immediately shifted up a few overtones in consciousness into a direct realization of the stated purpose for the day—to feel nature come alive and to see the presence of Spirit in everything.

Was this the proof from the angels for which I had asked? We had talked earlier in the week about how higher-dimensional "space brothers" can and do come down to our level and take whatever form is appropriate in the moment to greet us.

The next morning at breakfast was a time for final connections and good-byes, as most of the participants had a morning flight to catch.

The conversation at our table centered on a couple who were expecting a child in the next couple of weeks, and who were planning to do an underwater birth. I offered my full support and expressed the enormous value of allowing the umbilical cord to remain intact for up to four hours after birth, allowing the infant a chance to learn how to breathe rather than having the first breath forced upon him or her. Everyone at the table listened with total interest. They asked questions and soon I found myself in the middle of a discussion outlining the many benefits of rebirthing.

There was one woman at the far end of the table who had said little but was taking it all in. Suddenly, she came out with "Can we do a session now?" Doing a session was *absolutely* the furthest thing from my mind, it hadn't even remotely come into my awareness. So I replied, "I don't see how it's possible, we need privacy and we have to be checked out of our rooms by noon." She said, "Yes, but it's only ten o'clock now." I could sense her love and total intention, and I realized that I could not possibly say no. I was also beginning to sense something coming down from higher levels.

During the course of the workshop many people were going through various levels of intense emotional release. I had witnessed many times a phenomenon with which I had become very familiar—people going into spontaneous rebirthing sessions in the moment of that release. The medical establishment calls this experience hyperventilation and, not knowing what is really happening, usually intervenes to stop it. I had seen this many times before in rebirthing workshops and of course, in these settings, there was always a rebirther present to be with and guide the person to a completed energy cycle using the vehicle of their own breath. The results were always powerful and positive.

But here at this workshop, there were no rebirthers other than myself and one other person. Equally important, there was no agreement for it. I had experienced some frustration because I knew I had something that was very powerful and was needed and wanted, but there was no space for it. I had no one's permission to serve in this manner and hence could not do it.

I also knew that rebirthing was a vehicle that could be used to send people to tremendous new heights after they had completed the workshop. That is, I knew this in theory, but I had not yet put it into practice. It had to be tested.

So here was a perfect candidate, open and willing. Our rebirthing session totally confirmed what I knew. She was embraced by and clearly felt the presence of ascended masters and her angels. Then she felt herself regressing to an infant of three months, then into the womb, and regressing even further into the Great Void. From there she came back into the womb, experienced birth and grew back to the infant of three months. In the process, she had been "reborn" into the full awareness of her total connection with all life. Together we experienced a sense of love and unity that is far beyond words to describe.

Not only did this experience complete the entire workshop for me, it validated what I had known but had not yet proven. It also served to show me beyond any possible doubt that a higher-self connection had been made, that this had all been orchestrated from higher dimensional levels. The best analogy I can give is that if you are properly prepared, rebirthing is like being initiated in the Great Pyramid.

This rebirthing session led to my final completion—knowing, beyond any doubt whatsoever, that I was to become a "Flower of Life" facilitator and that I was to combine this work with my rebirthing practice. I knew, however, from the moment I first heard it from Drunvalo in a previous telephone conversation, I had also noticed that some doubts had crept in. I was in the midst of the healing process that I have described in this book.

As my doubts melted away, I was left with the full presence of my true purpose as a higher-dimensional master here to co-create heaven on Earth. I say this only to serve as a reminder to you of how great you are. The Spirit of God is in every one of us, just look in another's eyes. The time to remember this is now!

23

What Does It All Mean?

So what does this all mean? First of all, remember that nothing in this book is true—but it is exactly how things are.

Let me talk about what it does *not* mean. It does not mean that we can count on technology to get us out of our current situation. The ultimate technology is the external merkaba. That is the message of Cydonia.

Our increasing dependence on technology is what created our problem in the first place. In fact, the more technologically advanced we are, the more ignorant we are becoming. We are becoming increasingly separated from the One Spirit and we are weakening.

We become weaker when we keep giving away our power to technology, in other words, to external objects. We then become dependent upon these objects and soon get to the point where we can't do anything for ourselves. We also become habituated to obeying outside authority.

Instead of following outside authority (following instructions), the guiding principle of the new consciousness is to operate from our own authority. This means following the Spirit within without hesitation. As we learn to do this, we will discover that we already have everything we need—it is all within.

Furthermore, we will be guided t
exactly the right time and to meet
encounter. The best example I can
how this book came to be.

Because I was following Spirit with
thing has worked perfectly.

My initial motivation was to master this mate s
own sake. One day a new rebirthing client named Ri rd
Grossinger came to me. Richard just happens to run the publishing company that brought out Richard Hoagland's book,
The Monuments of Mars.

This book, of course, was right in the area of my greatest
interest. My natural tendency, then, was to tell Richard what
I knew about Mars. Shortly thereafter he asked me if I wanted
to write this book.

A few months later, Richard introduced me to his nine-
teen-year-old daughter Miranda. We talked about Mars,
aliens, secret governments, and so on. Afterwards Richard
asked her what she thought, and her comment was, "Well,
of course nothing he said was true, but it's exactly how things
are."

Since I do not operate a computer (I don't even type), it
was clearly necessary to enlist someone's help with the book
project. Enter Lois Cheesman who has proven many times
over to be the perfect partner in this venture.

Then I met a new friend, Alfred Lee, who offered to do
some of the geometrical drawings for me on his computer.
He was able to do them better and in a fraction of the time
that it had taken me to do them by hand.

This is how it works. As we follow Spirit, everything falls
into place effortlessly.

The most advanced civilizations in the galaxy have nothing, own nothing, outside of themselves. They can do anything they want, and without external objects.

Even if we do create external machines, we somehow have to get to the point where we can do what the machine does ourselves.

That is the direction in which we are headed. As we move from third- to fourth-dimensional consciousness—that is, from limitation or victim consciousness into mastery of divine expression—we are learning that we do have everything we need within. Our next leap in consciousness will be to go inside and discover it for ourselves.

The ultimate expression of this internal source is the merkaba. The vast majority of life in the galaxy uses the internal merkaba—they need nothing outside of themselves. They inhabit their own living time-space vehicle and have everything they need.

Soon, we will join them.

For information regarding "Flower of Life" and "Nothing to Something" workshops, rebirthing, and to receive a list of available books, tapes (including a guided merkaba meditation tape), and videos, write to:

Bob Frissell
c/o North Atlantic Books
P.O. Box 12327
Berkeley, CA 94712

Website: www.bobfrissell.com

Please include a self-addressed, stamped envelope.

INDEX

Something in This Book Is True ...

by Bob Frissell
ISBN: 1-883319-65-X
$14.95 trade paper
245 pp., illustrations

"In his companion book to *Nothing in This Book Is True, But It's Exactly How Things Are*, Bob Frissell once again delves into some controversial issues: earth changes, pole shifts, the secret government, UFOs, extraterrestrials, ascended masters, and multidimensional happenings, as he pulls together a wide variety of teachings— everything from Leonard Orr's rebirthing to sacred geometry to the merkaba, a kind of time/space self-generated magnetic field. In other words, it's a roller-coaster ride kind of book, one that clearly deserves Frissell's own warning—'Readers, put on your seat belts!'

"Much of what Frissell has to say is amazing, especially material relating to walk-in Drunvalo Melchizedek, ascended master Thoth, and the 'true history of the world.' While the book emphasizes the importance of seeing 'the whole picture,' the title itself begs the question—just what is true: what is real? Your belief system will almost certainly be tested (and perhaps stretched) by reading this book. One thing's for sure: it's certainly not a dull ride."

—Dawn Baumann Brunke, *Alaska Wellness*

You Are a Spiritual Being Having a Human Experience

by Bob Frissell
ISBN: 1-58394-033-2
$15.95 trade paper
160 pp., illustrations

Frissell writes freely about the spiritual and philosophical implications of the astonishing topics in his previous two books, showing how we can recover our birthright as spiritual beings. Frissell, certified Rebirther and seeker, has created a grand synthesis of practical insight, eternal wisdom, historical fact, and provocative speculation.

In *You Are a Spiritual Being Having a Human Experience* he invites us to entertain:

- How we can shift our identity from being a human victim to being a spiritual master;
- How the Unity of Being is the hidden meaning of all world religions;
- How a secret code discovered by Israeli scientists in the first five books of the Bible may contain the entire contents of the Akashic Record;
- How a genetically mutated race of special children called the "Indigos" are already present on Earth to lead us to higher levels of consciousness;
- How we may already passed into the fourth dimension.
- All this plus more news about the Sirians, the Martians, the Australian Aborigines, contemporary Mayans, and the present-day survivors from the fall of Atlantis.

Bob Frissell at the Atlanta Whole Life Expo

Audiotape, $12
Frissell recounts his story of how three major events changed his life forever. Topics include rebirthing, emotional body training, prana, integration, Babaji, and various Earth change prophecies.

Seeing Beyond

Set of two audiotapes, $16
Frissell and talk show hostess Bonnie Coleen discuss healing, prana, rebirthing, death and reincarnation, UFOs, and the dimensional shift.

Nothing to Something

VHS tape, $24.95, 1997
An autobiographical video chronicling Bob Frissell's journey that led to the writing of *Nothing in This Book Is True, But It's Exactly How Things Are* and *Something in This Book Is True . . .*, Babaji, Thoth, Ramtha, Leonard Orr, Drunvalo Melchizedek, UFOs, secret governments, and more.

Other Related Titles

Note: The following pages include other titles on related topics published by North Atlantic Books/Frog, Ltd. They were written independently and do not necessarily have the involvement or endorsement of the author of this book.

Portals and Corridors:
A Visionary Guide to Hyperspace

By Monica Szu-Whitney and Gary Whitney
Foreword by Terence McKenna
ISBN: 1-883319-76-5
$18.95 trade paper
352 pp., full color drawings
The beings in this book lie far from us in actual time-space and are hard to see, but their destinies and ours are intertwined, and they bear critical messages for all inhabitants of the Earth.

The Book of Theanna:
In the Lands That Follow Death

By Ellias and Theanna Lonsdale
ISBN: 1-883319-37-4
$16.95 trade paper
344 pp.
Before she died, Theanna (then Sara Lonsdale) developed a means to continue communication with her husband Ellias. *The Book of Theanna* contains Ellias' daily transcriptions of her words through Death's doors. In the course of these epistles she discusses the scenery of Death; the denials and delusions of the recently dead; and the nature of sexuality, violence, and power.

Inside Star Vision:
Planetary Awakening and Self-Transformation

By Ellias and Theanna Lonsdale
ISBN: 1-55643-324-7
$16.95 trade paper
208 pp., charts

The real astrology far transcends conventional charts and horoscopes and seeks our essence in the vast dimensions of an actual universe, a universe of hyperspace, reincarnation, karma, and the spiritual initiation of souls. Lonsdale delineates the years 2000, 2001, 2002, 2003, 2004, 2005, and 2006, and in a daring and profound act of spiritual writing, he sets the cosmic terms for the imminent transformation of humanity through an opening of the door between the two most separated realms of all, life and death.

The Monuments of Mars:
A City on the Edge of Forever, 2001 edition

By Richard C. Hoagland
Preface by Richard Grossinger
ISBN: 1-58394-054-5
$29.95 trade paper
712 pp., 80-page glossy photo insert

"Either these features on Mars are natural and this investigation is a complete waste of time, or they are artificial and this is one of the most important discoveries of our entire existence on Earth. If they are artificial it is imperative that we figure them out, because they 'do not belong there.' Their presence may be trying very hard to tell us something extraordinary."—Richard C. Hoagland

Breaking the Death Habit:
The Science of Everlasting Life

By Leonard Orr
Preface by Bob Frissell
ISBN: 1-883319-68-4
$14.95 trade paper
166 pp.

"Leonard Orr has the ability to alter reality. If you enter into a relation with him with any degree of sincerity, you will be mutated. Stuff is going to come up in his presence—anything that is less pure than he is—and you are going to have to address it. Reading this book is entering into a relationship with him."—Bob Frissell

Architects of the Underworld:
Unriddling Atlantis, Anomalies of Mars,
and the Mystery of the Sphinx

By Bruce Rux
ISBN: 1-883319-46-3
$18.95 trade paper
540 pp., illustrations

Rux reveals the links between extraterrestrial phenomena and the legendary civilization of Atlantis, the Egyptian pyramids, the Sphinx, and the anomalies on the canal-coursed surface of Mars, including the controversial "Face."

Hollywood Versus the Aliens: The Motion Picture Industry's Participation in UFO Disinformation

By Bruce Rux
ISBN: 1-883319-61-7
$19.95 trade paper
724 pp., b&w photos
Early '50s movies like *The Thing from Another World* and *The Day the Earth Stood Still* show UFOlogical facts that only government sources could have known at the time. From there the book goes on to discuss recent releases and the ongoing depictions of aliens and UFOs, right up to *Independence Day, Men in Black,* and *Mars Attacks!*

The Deepening Complexity of Crop Circles: Scientific Research and Urban Legends

By Eltjo Haselhoff, Ph.D.
ISBN: 1-58394-046-4
174 pp., full color throughout
In his full-color book the author skillfully addresses the most compelling anomalies that define this evolving mystery, including: the formations' tendency to appear suddenly, in time spans as short as thirty minutes; the presence of unexpected geometric laws and proofs in some formations; the presence of "stunned" or exploded insects; unusual glass "microspheres" and other unexpected deposits in affected grains; and the inextricable connection between crop circles and oft-reported and filmed "balls of light."

Alien Apocalypse 2006

By Kathy Glass
Illustrated by Spain
and Harry S. Robins
ISBN: 1-883319-63-3
$10.95 trade paper
A comic book—fully illustrated throughout
To Beings in a time-free realm who watch us believe in the delusion of outer time, it must be hard to trust the evidence of their own eyes as they fully grasp where this belief leads us ... "This is the one, my friends. It really does exist ... They throw their wealth away with both hands. But time opens through not one, but many paths into timelessness. Their world is close to its 'end.'"

Channeling:
Investigations on Receiving Information
from Paranormal Sources

By Jon Klimo
Foreword by Charles Tart
ISBN: 1-55643-248-8
$19.95 trade paper
496 pp.
"... the sacred text on channeling."—*Newsweek*

Multidimensional Mind:
Remote Viewing in Hyperspace

By Jean Millay
Foreword by Stanley Krippner
ISBN: 1-55643-306-9
256 pp., b&w and color photos
"*Multidimensional Mind* is the most comprehensive and scientifically authoritative book I have ever read. It is a book suited to readers who are curious about telepathy, the unexplained, the mysteries of the mind, and brainpower."

—Uri Geller

WWW.NORTHATLANTICBOOKS.COM